T0277623

Beautiful
PEAKS

Publisher
Balthazar Pagani

Graphic design
Davide Canesi / PEPE *nymi*

WS White Star Publishers® is a registered trademark property of White Star s.r.l.

© 2023 White Star s.r.l.
Piazzale Luigi Cadorna, 6
20123 Milan, Italy
www.whitestar.it

Translation: Richard Pierce
Editing: Phillip Gaskill

All rights reserved. No part of this publication may be reproduced, stored in a retrieval system, or transmitted in any form or by any means, including electronic, mechanical, photocopying, recording, or otherwise, without written permission from the publisher.

ISBN 978-88-544-1995-7
1 2 3 4 5 6 27 6 25 24 23

Printed in China

~ NICOLA BALOSSI RESTELLI ~

Beautiful

PEAKS

Famous peaks
that hold
great records,
mountains with

a glorious
history, and
places of great
spirituality

WHITE STAR PUBLISHERS

. CONTENTS .

PROFOUND ALTITUDES 7

DENALI
Alaska, USA 13

MAUNA LOA
Hawaii, USA 19

HALF DOME
California, USA 25

RORAIMA
Venezuela/Brazil/Guyana 33

ALPAMAYO
Peru 41

HUAYNA PICCHU
Peru 49

LICANCABUR
Chile/Bolivia 57

CERRO TORRE
Argentina/Chile 65

KIRKJUFELL
Iceland 77

MONT BLANC
France/Italy 85

MATTERHORN
Italy/Switzerland................. 95

THE CIME DI LAVAREDO
Italy 105

KILIMANJARO
Tanzania......................... 115

TABLE MOUNTAIN
South Africa..................... 123

ARARAT
Turkey........................... 131

DAMĀVAND
Iran 139

NANGA PARBAT
Pakistan......................... 147

LAILA PEAK
Pakistan......................... 157

K2
Pakistan/China................... 165

KAILASH
China............................ 175

EVEREST
Nepal/China...................... 185

AMA DABLAM
Nepal 195

FUJI
Japan............................ 205

ULURU (or AYERS ROCK)
Australia........................ 215

PROFOUND ALTITUDES

Impetuous, frenetic, increasingly engulfed in the deadening habitat of our various screens, we risk losing contact with the time and place of the present.

Yet there is a force that travels stubbornly in the opposite direction and is able to overturn our perspective: the voice of nature, with all its nuances, from an almost imperceptible whisper to a peremptory order. This voice reminds us that we are merely a speck of dust in the universe as well as fortunate creatures who can enjoy its immensity. Often what speaks to us are the landscapes, or the bewitching and inaccessible sea, capable of lulling us tenderly or annihilating us with a mere movement—salty, bitter, arid, and solitary, yet teeming with life.

A mountain is not much different: large and benign, radiant in its splendor and demure in its hidden depths. It is as attractive as the sensation of vertigo or at times an embrace, but also distant and almost cruel in its manifest indifference—generous, quite willing to share its resources and beauty, yet impregnable, the sole master of itself.

While planning this book, we realized that every mountain is a rich and many-faceted world that is almost impossible to encapsulate; but all the same, we set out to trace out a portrait, a suggestion that would generate emotions and thoughts. Unable to discern exactly where a mountain begins, we started off with the peaks, the most conspicuous and profound part, the farthest from the bowels of Earth. Seen by everyone, the summit is more than a mere objective; it is the concrete form of the very concept of an objective, and is also abstract and symbolic. The summit is observed from a distance and is dreamt of at length; it is studied and loved, and sometimes becomes an obsession. Sometimes a long wait and laborious preparation are required. Yet the very moment the flag is planted, it is already time to leave, because, everything considered, a peak makes sense only when viewed at a certain distance; once on the summit, you immediately realize that the summit itself can no longer be seen. What remains of so much ambition is only a photograph or two and a sandwich eaten in a hurry.

The mountains we have chosen are different and many-faceted, located at the four corners of the world and associated with great and romantic stories that are often mysterious. Their energy, which can be perceived firsthand or by means of photos and drawings, has often inspired mystical thoughts about the sky and beyond. For each mountain there is a "sketch," consisting of only a few lines of description in order to let the photographs speak for themselves.

In most cases, we have not been on the summits, but have been enchanted by their hypnotic shapes and immersed in the worlds below them; we were amazed, well aware that every peak is an aspiration, an idea that makes sense even if you never manage to achieve it. Drawing contrasts is inevitable, because Man's conquests are indomitable and distant; yet this distance is the echo of something both intimate and primordial that is an intrinsic part of our makeup. At bottom, the purpose of this book is to plant seeds in the souls of those who already "live and breathe" mountains, as well as those who know little about them, because we believe there are two categories of persons: those who love mountains, and those who love them but are not yet aware of this.

DENALI
(formerly MOUNT McKINLEY)

Altitude: 20,310 ft. (6190 m) a.s.l.
Prominence: 20,194 ft. (6155 m)
Topographic isolation: 4,621.1 mi. (7,436.9 km)
Coordinates: latitude 63°04'10" N; longitude 151°00'24" E
Location: Talkeetna

A QUESTION OF GOLD

A part of the Alaska Range, in the middle of Denali National Park and Preserve, Denali consists of two granite peaks with a permanent cover of snow. The South Summit is the highest on the continent, while the elevation of the north one is 19,470 ft. (5934 m) above sea level. The mountain includes five large glaciers. Despite its wide and gradual profile, Denali is truly monumental, partly thanks to its prominence, or elevation with respect to the terrain it lies on, a tableland with an average elevation of about 2297 ft. (700 m) above sea level.

The native Athabaskan population called the peak Denali—the "great one" or "tall one"—while the other, lower peak was called "Denali's wife." The culture of those who managed to inhabit this inhospitable area was based on respect for, and veneration of, nature, which was perhaps the only way of thinking that could make it possible for them to settle there.

There is nothing surprising about the fact that the Americans, who had purchased Alaska from the Russians in 1867, were not especially respectful of these traditions and had no misgivings about changing the name of this venerable mountain to Mount McKinley to honor the 25th president of the United States, William McKinley, a Republican and veteran of the American Civil War who was assassinated shortly after beginning his second term of office, in September 1901. He had never been to the mountain but had influenced the gold rush in Alaska, which led to increasing the percentage of gold in coins and thus its value.

IN THE WILD

~

Who knows what it thinks, or indeed whether it thinks at all. Who knows if it deigns to pay any attention to human matters, at least those that pertain to it.

Who knows if the tallest summit in North America was stirred when it regained its ancient name during the Obama presidency in 2015, after a long and rocky dispute triggered by the 1975 decision of the Alaska Board on Geographic Names to change the name on a federal level, which was vigorously opposed by the governors of Ohio, where William McKinley was born.

The rationale behind this dissent cannot be understood by humans, not to speak of the mountain itself, which observes almost the entire world from on high.

Who knows if the mountain trembled when faced with the torment endured by Christopher McCandless (alias Alexander Supertramp, whose true story inspired the movie *Into the Wild* adapted from the book of the same title by Jon Krakauer), who suffered terribly in this hostile region before finding his true self in the ancestral link with nature and, just at this crowning moment, died from a poisonous berry. Perhaps the objective eye of the mountain was filled with tears. We'll never know. But we do know the effect made by the peak that is the undisputed dominator of North America, more or less equidistant from Himalaya and the great mountain ranges of South America, and more than 4350 miles (7000 km) from any higher peak. An atmosphere of mute respect spreads from those altitudes to the entire surroundings, a powerful return to Man's humble submission when faced with Mother Nature, an order of things we are often unmindful of, trapped as we are in our asphyxiating and egocentric metropolises.

THE MISTAKES
AND THE CONQUEST

&

THE DENALI SUMMIT IS NOT FOR EVERYBODY. TO THIS DAY, AROUND HALF THE ATTEMPTED ASCENTS HAVE ENDED WITH RELINQUISHMENT OR FAILURE, ABOVE ALL DUE TO THE PRO-HIBITIVE TEMPERATURE (AN AVERAGE OF 40 DEGREES BELOW ZERO), HEAVY SNOWFALL, STRONG WINDS, AND FEW HOURS OF SUNLIGHT IN WINTER, WHICH, TAKEN AS A WHOLE, LIMIT THE FAVORABLE PERIOD FOR THE ASCENT TO THE MONTHS OF MAY AND JUNE.

It is not surprising that the conquest of the peak was achieved only after a series of errors. In 1906, during his third attempt, the explorer Frederick Cook declared that he had reached the summit and described his feat in a book that included photographic documentation. Unfortunately, later on it was proven that he had not been on the right peak, but on another one 6.2 mi. (10 km) away. This controversy finally ended only in 1956, when two mountaineers identified the exact spot immortalized by Cook's photograph. The second failure is certainly more entertaining, at least in regard to the descriptions of the event handed down

to us. In 1910, a group of miners, during an evening of heavy drinking in Fairbanks, decided to make the ascent to that fascinating yet inaccessible peak. The owner of the saloon and a whisky dealer took the group's bragging so seriously that they offered to finance the "outing." Much to their surprise, however, even after their drinking jag, the miners remembered what they had said the previous evening and declared that they had no intention to renege their plan. So their "expedition" took on shape in earnest, because one does not go back on his word, especially if uttered in an outburst of mischief. The ascent didn't go too badly but was not a total success: the miners, much too eager to drink to their achievement, had planted a flag on the smaller peak, while below them the sponsors tried in vain to warn them about this: but the latter, intoxicated not only with self-esteem, mistook those desperate gestures as a manifestation of irrepressible joy and triumph. In 1913, another expedition, led by Hudson Stuck, followed the same route— which had become even more difficult due to a powerful earthquake that had struck the area the preceding summer—and finally, with the aid of the sun, managed to reach the tallest summit in North America.

MAUNA LOA

Altitude: 13,679 ft. (4169 m) a.s.l.
Prominence: 7079 ft. (2158 m)
Topographic isolation: not available
Coordinates: latitude 19°28'46" N; longitude 155°36'9" W
Location: Island of Hawaii

THE MOON ON EARTH

The paradox of modern Man: confined and repressed as he is in narrow, artificial spaces, he is stupefied when in the presence of anything more uncontaminated. We often find ourselves saying "What a lovely spot, it doesn't even seem we are in . . ." (followed by "such-and-such a city"). In some cases, the smell of wild solitude is so strong that we cannot bear it, so we even go so far as to think that certain places do not belong to this world because they are *too natural*. We have the impression of being on the Moon or Mars, because we cannot hear the continuous and insistent background noise of human traffic: we are so accustomed to it that we suffer when it is lacking. In fact, what seems to be an unknown planet is nothing more or less than our Earth in one of its many manifestations, which are so domineering and strong that they torment us.

This is the landscape of Mauna Loa, as unsettling as one can imagine. Located on the principal island of Hawaii, and with an estimated volume of 18,000 cu. mi. (75,000 cu. km), it is the largest active volcano in the world. To get a more compelling idea of its size, if we include its submarine flanks—16,400 ft. (ca. 5000 m) deep to the sea floor—this massif is 30,085 ft. (9170 m) high, thus taller than Mt. Everest. The barren and wild landscape reminds one of the surface of the Moon, but this crater is actually as "terrestrial" as can be, closely connected to the boiling depths of our planet. Mauna Loa, the Long Mountain, emerged around 400,000 years ago, and still makes its voice heard at irregular intervals. Its lava, very poor in silica and therefore only slightly viscous, has erupted for hundreds of centuries, creating the volcano's shield shape with gradual slopes.

A LONG PAUSE

~

It is estimated that from 1843 to the present, Mauna Loa has erupted 33 times. There are apocalyptic 19th-century descriptions of these events, in which the rivers of lava flow swiftly toward the sea, sweeping away the animals, houses, and persons in their path. The year 1950 marked the most violent episode in human memory: the lava flooded the village of Ho-'okena-mauka, destroying roads and houses but fortunately sparing human lives (there is spectacular black-and-white film footage of this event). Earthquakes and tsunamis connected to the eruptions have wrought the most serious damage. For example, in 1868 a huge landslide and an atypical wave caused by quakes killed 70 persons and destroyed many homes. Yet from 1984 to 2021 this volcano gave no signs of life—the longest dormancy ever recorded in its history. Then in the autumn of 2022, seismic activity increased in an ominous manner, followed by a new and extensive eruption in late November. Now, although this type of extremely fluid magma rarely produces dangerous explosive phenomena, potential risks must not be underestimated, as occurred during the 2022 event, which instead of causing panic led to what could be called "eruption tourism."

In any case, Mauna Loa boasts an absolutely unique combination of altitude and topographic isolation; consequently, a meteorological station was installed there in order to supply extremely reliable data on the global concentration of carbon dioxide.

THE MYTHS

∾

THERE ARE MANY STORIES, MOST REVOLVING AROUND PELE, THE GODDESS OF FIRE WHOSE POWER CAN BE CONSIDERED TO EXTEND TO INCLUDE THE CAPACITY TO GENERATE AND DESTROY, OR TO REGENERATE BY MEANS OF DESTRUCTION IN A CYCLICAL PROCESS CLOSELY CONNECTED TO THE POWER OF THE ELEMENTS. IT IS SAID THAT SHE CAME FROM TAHITI TO ESCAPE FROM THE FURY OF HER SISTER NA-MAKA-O-KA-HA'I, THE GODDESS OF THE OCEAN, WHOSE HUSBAND PELE HAD SEDUCED. THE SAME DANGEROUS ITINERARY WAS LATER FOLLOWED BY THE FUTURE HAWAIIAN POPULATION, WHICH MIGRATED TOGETHER WITH ITS ANIMALS AND SEEDS ON A HUGE CANOE, FLEEING FROM THE LOCAL PRIESTS WHO ENFORCED HUMAN SACRIFICES IN HONOR OF THE GOD ORO.

Pele can take on the likeness of an irresistibly beautiful girl or of a ferocious and choleric witch, just as her indomitable temperament can create miracles or disasters, depending on her mood. For example, once, in order to punish a young village chieftain who had rejected her amorous advances (he was already married), this powerful goddess triggered a tremendous eruption that the locals escaped only by going into the sea in their canoes. It seems that to this day, the mere recollection of that humiliation has caused many eruptions. On the other hand, every period of devastation is followed by one of fertility and rebirth, and in fact this goddess is often invoked to overcome periods of stagnation and change destiny. Further proof of Pele's ambivalence is her habit of sending a white dog to warn the population of an imminent eruption. Peridot, a light green gem that is quite common on the island, is considered made of Pele's tears, and gathering and possessing it is totally forbidden. In fact, tradition has it that misfortune strikes those who dare take any type of stone from the Mauna Loa volcano. Although not everyone takes this seriously, it is a proven fact that many visitors send back to the island the souvenirs they have rashly stolen because they are convinced that the latter have given rise to a series of misfortunes. In short, you'd better not trifle with the goddess Pele.

HALF DOME

Altitude: 8838 ft. (2694 m) a.s.l.
Prominence: 1360 ft. (414.5 m)
Topographic isolation: not available
Coordinates: latitude 37°44'45.73" N; longitude 119°31'58.58" W
Location: Yosemite National Park

A TALON IN THE SKY

It looks like a creature, a sort of chipped petrified dolphin photographed while about to emerge and take flight toward the sky and beyond. Perhaps it resembles even more the profile of a bird of prey, but we all know that peaks are like clouds: everyone sees what they want to see. What's more, our perception changes quite a lot according to our observation point, so this peak may easily resemble a squirrel, a crow, or even a penguin. This block of cleft granite rises up right in the middle of Yosemite Park, and two fixed steel cables allow a large number of persons to reach the summit after about a day's hike along trails. Half Dome is at once static and dynamic, since it changes continuously. In the first place, the light paints it in a different way at different hours and days. Secondly, the dome has had plenty of time to acquire its varied shapes, as it is part of an immense block of magmatic rock sculpted for millions of years by water and glaciers. Here, where pointed peaks alternate with lush valleys among rivers, falls, and millennial trees, in an ecosystem that has been conserved thanks to the area's status as a national park, human presence has a history of more than 3,000 years. And the natives, especially the Ahwahnechee, lived in these areas for a long time before being exterminated and subjugated by colonists from the mid-19th century on. Fortunately, the enlightened initiative of some persons—above all, the naturalist John Muir—triggered the process that led to the definitive establishment of the Yosemite National Park in 1916, thus saving this jewel from being ruined by human impact.

THE CHALLENGES

~

Half Dome lends itself to contemplation from a distance, so much so that the 18th-century geologist Josiah Whitney, after several vain attempts at climbing to the summit, stated flatly that it would never be treaded on by a human foot. Today he would certainly be surprised to see the slow daily procession of hundreds of persons making the climb that was precluded to him, and he would be even more amazed at the idea that other, much more difficult and rougher trails would be "violated" over the years.

While it was George Anderson who left the first footprint on the summit, achieving this thanks to iron bolts he placed at a 45° angle in the granitic plate that today doesn't seem impassable but certainly was at that time, the ascents of the other faces were more complicated and thus took place at a later date. Only in 1946 did John Salathé, of Swiss origin, and Alex Nelson precede six rivals in their rope-climb ascent of the southwest face. As is often the case, this is a question of having the proper equipment, in particular bolts; theirs were long and thin but very resistant and could be planted in cracks that other bolts could not penetrate. The two climbers needed 150 of

them; and after spending a night on the face, they completed the ascent.

There remains the northwest face, which is impassable only for those who don't have enough imagination. It was the ideal theater for a rivalry of epic magnitude. Royal Robbins was a formidable climber, taciturn, thoughtful, and with intellectual aspirations, while his nemesis Warren Harding was an out-and-out devil, addicted especially to alcohol and women, an absolute non-conformist and troublemaker but also able to concentrate all his controversial energy and confront every mountain with fury and determination. The two rivals made an ascent together in 1955, but it ended badly. Here again, the evolution in the making of bolts was fundamental: those that were used by Robbins and two fellow climbers were even longer and thinner, and allowed them to overcome the challenge in five days, spending the nights on the face. Who should be waiting for them on the summit but Harding, who had not been invited to make the ascent and was green with envy, and who had taken the normal route in order to congratulate as well as insult his archenemy. The very same anger led Harding to successfully climb the face of El Capitan—but that is another story.

ON THE WING

∾

THE DATE ITSELF TELLS THE WHOLE STORY: 7 JULY 1977 (7-7-77), WHEN THREE DAREDEVIL AND BEARDED HIPPIES DECIDED TO CHALLENGE FATE AND THE STRICT PARK RANGERS. A BIT LIKE THE FAMOUS *MAN ON WIRE* OF THE TWIN TOWERS, PHILIPPE PETIT, RICH PICCIRILLI HAD TO ORGANIZE THE EXPLOIT AS IF IT WERE A BANK ROBBERY.

The approach to the summit with concealed equipment took two nights, including an attack on the part of a bear that complicated matters. But by the morning of that day, everything was ready, and the three friends jumped from the crown of Half Dome on their hang glider. Time seemed to stand still, as is fitting when Man realizes one of his ancestral dreams: to be able to fly. After a bit, Piccirilli's companions jumped off with a parachute—which opened just in time—while Piccirilli glided gently over the trees. Of course, the uncompromising rangers arrested him a few hours later, but the grainy images in the documentary that describes this feat leave no room for doubts: it was worthwhile.

MOUNT RORAIMA

Altitude: 9186 ft. (2800 m) a.s.l.
Prominence: 7671 ft. (2338 m)
Topographic isolation: not available
Coordinates: latitude 5°10'59" N; longitude 60°45'59" W
Location: Paraitepuy, Bolivar, Venezuela

A HIGH-ALTITUDE ISLAND

It's not what one expects a mountain to look like. The classical point on the summit is lacking, and this enormous tableland right in the middle of the pluvial forest resembles for the most part an immense ghost raft suspended above a sea of fog. But there is absolutely nothing ghostly about it, because it teems with life, life that is unique the world over for its wealth and preservation of endemic species. This rock formation, typical of the area, is called *tepui* in the local idiom: that is, "House of the Gods," which gives us an idea of the sacred aura that surrounds it. Roraima is an island about half as high as Manhattan, defended by a precipitous cliff 1312 ft. (400 m) tall on all sides. The tepui began to develop about two billion years ago, and its inaccessibility, together with its microclimate, which is quite different from the hot and humid one below it, has preserved these zones from all forms of contamination, thus making them precious theaters of an extremely long evolution of indigenous species. Carnivorous plants, orchids, and Roraima black frogs that do not hop but curl up into a ball and roll when in danger, are only tiny examples of what is to be found on this immense block of sandstone and quartzite sculpted by time and atmospheric agents. The almost-daily rainfall and the resultant dissolution of the limestone on the formation have helped to create rocky forests, as well as potholes that have become unique "biological nurseries." This small, ancient, and impregnable world boasts *El labirinto*, a maze of caves and fissures in the rock, and Crystal Valley, whose entire quartz surface shines, while a triangular landmark lies at the so-called Triple Point, where the borders of Venezuela, Guyana, and Brazil converge.

ROYAL EXPEDITIONS

~

The native populations, in particular the Pemon, who still live in the extensive forest areas below the mountain, have always considered the tepuis as sacred sites and have never dreamt of violating Mt. Roraima, which was described for the first time to Europeans by Sir Walter Raleigh, who on behalf of Queen Elizabeth I explored many areas of South and North America and initiated their colonization. In 1595, this piratical adventurer—who was decapitated for treason during the reign of King James I—observed the mountain from below and included it in his controversial travel diary. But the first documented conquest of the tepui took place much later, in December 1884, with the expedition of Sir Everard Ferdinand im Thurn. Gifted with multifarious talents, as befits a pioneer, he was a botanist, photographer, and administrator of several British colonies, the first person to set foot on this paradisiacal tableland of biodiversity who then published precious documentation regarding the bold mission financed by the Royal Geographical Society.

DIVINE PUNISHMENT

∾

FOR THE NATIVES, MOUNT RORAIMA IS THE MOTHER OF ALL WATERS, AND THE CIRCUMSTANCES OF HER BIRTH WILL SOUND VERY FAMILIAR TO PEOPLE IN THE WESTERN WORLD. IN AN UNDETERMINED PAST, IN FACT, THIS AREA WAS A LUXURIANT PLAIN, ABOUNDING WITH STREAMS AND RIVERS AS WELL AS FRUIT THAT A BENEVOLENT NATURE HAD PROVIDED TO THE INHABITANTS. HOWEVER, THERE WAS ONE SIMPLE AND FUNDAMENTAL CONDITION IMPOSED BY THE GOD PAABA: NO ONE WAS TO EAT THE FRUIT OF A SACRED BANANA PLANT THAT HAD GROWN IN THIS LAND.

Simple, isn't it? The answer is no, because humans do not get along with harmony, and so the first profaner looking for trouble defied this prohibition and felled the tree in order to steal a bunch of this precious fruit. Naturally, a violent cloudburst broke—Paaba's tears of disappointment, or his punishment, or both, most probably—and put to flight most of the living creatures, while the abandoned land rose hundreds of yards above the forest level. The many streams and rivers that still descend from the rocky walls are considered a consequence of this movement.

The mysterious fascination of the Roraima area cannot fail to have an impact, and it became the setting for Sir Arthur Conan Doyle's novel *The Lost World*, filled with dinosaurs, which in turn inspired Michael Crichton's *Jurassic Park*. The supposition that prehistoric animals live there has not been confirmed, but one must point out that the area is, for the most part, yet to be explored.

ALPAMAYO

Altitude: 11,511 ft. (5947 m) a.s.l.
Prominence: 1467 ft. (447 m)
Topographic isolation: not available
Coordinates: latitude 8°52'45" S; longitude 77°39'13" W
Location: Huascarán National Park

THE MOST BEAUTIFUL

It is hard to resist the temptation to coin a sensational or almost rhetorical name for it, difficult to describe the amazing and hypnotic sensation one has when observing its almost perfect shape. And at bottom, it is not necessary to confute someone who has stated very simply that it is the loveliest mountain in the world—a status officially certified by UNESCO in 1966, for that matter. We could argue that the idea of the most beautiful mountain will often come to mind when reading this book, but must admit that we will inevitably think the same of Alpamayo. There is something unreal about this snowbound pyramid, yet it really exists. It is its magnetic appearance, rather than height, that makes it unique. The present name, consisting of the words *allpa* (earth) and *mayu* (river) in the Quechua language, actually refers to an agricultural zone at the foot of the mountain, while the upper part was named with a combination of *shuytu* (something like "long and thin") and *raju* ("snow-covered mountain"), hence Shuyturahu. Probably in the long run, the name that prevailed was the one that sounded better. Alpamayo is part of the Macizo de Santa Cruz massif in the northern zone of the Cordillera Blanca, a mountain chain 112 mi. (180 km) long consisting of more than 30 peaks over 19,685 ft. (6000 m) high, headed by Mount Huascarán, which is 22,205 ft. (6768 m) above sea level. A good portion of the Cordillera, so named because of the large number of glaciers, lies in the Huascarán National Park, established in 1975, which protects the environment and regulates the access fees.

A DIFFICULT CONQUEST

~

Despite its attractive air, this summit is not easily accessible; merely in order to fully appreciate it from below, one must tackle remarkably long and difficult routes. This aura of impregnability contributes to the continuity of its profound and stimulating fascination. Everyone who has been there describes it with due reverence and a sense of gratitude and respect in the highest and most spiritual meaning of these words, as if evoking a hard-won, longed-for, and unforgettable embrace.

In 1951, a French-Belgian expedition consisting of the mountaineers Jongen, Kogan, Leininger, and Lenoir opened a route on the northern crest and mistakenly believed they had reached the tallest peak. They announced their exploit with great pomp and ceremony, but it was soon clear that the summit they had conquered was only the lower, north peak. On the other hand, on 20 July 1957, Günter Hauser led a German rope team that made the first successful ascent of the summit by following a route on the southern crest.

THE ITALIAN ROUTE

∽

THERE IS A DOCUMENTARY THAT, PRESENTED WITH THE CALM AND RETRO TONE OF THE VOICE-OVERS OF FORMER TIMES AND THE TIMELESS MAGIC OF CINEMA, OFFERS A FINE DESCRIPTION OF THE MAGNIFICENT PERSONAL SIGNIFICANCE OF CHALLENGING A PEAK. VOCIFEROUS COMMENTS AND SENSATIONALISM ARE UNNECESSARY WHEN NARRATING WHAT IS TRULY GREAT. IN FACT, VERY LITTLE IS NEEDED: MERELY LET THE TRUE PROTAGONIST, THE MOUNTAIN, SPEAK FOR ITSELF—THE MOUNTAIN WHICH AT TIMES MAY AGREE TO BE CONQUERED BY THOSE TINY HUMAN ANTS CAPABLE OF STRIKING A BALANCE BETWEEN ALMOST ARROGANT AMBITION AND THE REQUIRED COMPETENCE, HUMILITY, AND PHYSICAL PREPARATION. THE REST IS UP TO DESTINY.

The ascent led by Casimiro Ferrari, originally from Lecco, with his fellow climbers Borgonovo, Castelnuovo, Liati, Negri, and Zoia (known as the Ragni di Lecco or Lecco Spiders), had been prepared down to the last detail. But if you add a 34-hour climb on a rock face 2297 ft. (700 m) high to an already long approach, as well as all the snags that might occur, it is easy to understand the major role played by chance, serendipity, or whatever else one wants to call it. In this juncture, the mountain said yes, and on the southwest wall the team opened a route no one else had ever climbed. It was the year 1975, and the route would remain known as the Ferrari Route. On the contrary, it was precisely on this route, in 2014, that a great tragedy took place. Four young alpinists from the Cantù area were only a step away from their dream of conquering the peak. Experience and preparation were on their side, as was their choice of the less-risky face, but in this case it was fortune that turned its back on them. When they were only a little more than a hundred yards from the summit, one of the two roped parties, consisting of Enrico Broggi and Matteo Tagliabue, who were not even thirty years old, was hit by an avalanche caused by the detachment of a snow ledge. The searches made by the two friends following them, Marco Ballerini and Giacomo Longhi, were in vain, as were the attempts of rescuers, who were obstructed in part by the adverse weather conditions.

HUAYNA PICCHU

Altitude: 8835 ft. (2693 m) a.s.l.
Prominence: 853 ft. (260 m)
Topographic isolation: not available
Coordinates: latitude 13°09'27" S; longitude 72°32'50" W
Location: Cuzco region

THE STAIRS OF DEATH

This peak is part of the East Cordillera of the Andes and is known as Young Mountain, as opposed to nearby Machu Picchu, or Old Mountain.

One cannot disregard the influence of Man in this setting. Our queries and amazement are based not so much on what the world offers us, but rather on the relationship with the works of our ancestors, which indisputably appear to blend more with the environment than most modern constructions.

Here everything is more pleasing to the eye; even the sharp edges of the mountain blunted by the greenery are comparable to breathtaking curves. And breath will certainly be difficult while going uphill, but it is well worth it, because Huayna Picchu is the tallest peak in this area and offers a unique view of

the gigantic Inca site clinging to the surrounding valleys.

The ascent to the summit, allowed to only 400 persons per day, is made via a long series of very steep and exposed steps that unsettles those who suffer from vertigo or claustrophobia, since a short part of the climb threads its way through a narrow and dark crevice in the granitic rock. There are no tall parapets or wide and comfortable steps, but the greatest danger are the social networks, which hypnotize visitors to such an extent that they brainlessly dash about to take a selfie, sometimes with tragic outcomes. Official sources state there has been no fatality that can be attributed to the "stairs of death." The most serious or lethal accidents have always been caused by appalling rashness.

ONE PEAK, MANY MYSTERIES

~

Obviously, it is useless to ask who was the first person to conquer this peak, but there is no lack of questions regarding the site. In fact, one could say that the mountain is a series of doubts and queries interspersed with some rational theories.

What is certain is that the Western world discovered the settlement of Machu Picchu in 1911 thanks to a Yale University professor, Hiram Bingham, who in turn owes thanks to a hint given by a generous local. The civilization we call Inca, after the name of the deified king—the son of the sun god Inti—and, by extension, of the ruling aristocracy, is brimming with fascinating aspects. It was a vast empire that at its acme—which was soon achieved thanks to its formidable military expansion—had a population of 10 million, embraced a territory that extended from the Andes in present-day Chile and Argentina as far as Ecuador, and boasted a vast network of roads and bridges. The lack of a system of writing adds mystery to the history of this civilization before the tragic encounter with the conquistadores. Again, there was also no coinage. The imposing taxation system was managed by means of a system of knotted strings that only a tiny élite was able to decipher and that were swiftly taken throughout the empire by a huge number of well-organized relay runners. While the Incas were prohibited from even looking into the eyes of the emperor Atahualpa, Francisco Pizarro had no qualms about capturing him, and later on had him executed with the garrote despite the huge ransom he had paid for his freedom. The Spanish pillaged and destroyed, and were followed by a series of other populations that had formerly been under Inca rule. The Spaniards' desecrating violence ceased only after this people had been totally subjugated, but their iconoclastic fury left intact the settlement of Machu Picchu, which had been abandoned—for reasons unknown. Although there are reasons to believe that populations of farmers had lived in this area long before the year 1000, the construction of the buildings probably dates to sometime after 1440, at the behest of the emperor Pachacuti, who founded the Inca empire. According to the most reliable theory, this settlement was a sort of summer residence for the emperor and an elite of dignitaries, although there are alternative hypotheses, such as the one that considers it the home of the sanctuary of the sun virgins, a supposition stemming from the discovery of a large number of female mummies. Besides the houses, Machu Picchu also has temples dedicated to natural elements, such as the one consecrated to the moon on the slopes of Huayna Picchu.

It would seem that these sites were abandoned spontaneously during the twilight of the Inca civilization, after which they sank into oblivion. In the period of their "rediscovery"—which, according to some scholars, should be backdated 44 years and attributed to the German Berns (but there is no real proof of this)— this land was cultivated silently by some farmers who still used an Incan canal for irrigation.

BETWEEN THE EARTH
AND THE SKY

∾

WE HAVE NO INFORMATION CONCERNING THE INCAS' BUILDING TECHNIQUES AND LOGISTICS OF TRANSPORT-ING MATERIAL, BUT THEIR KNOWLEDGE OF ENGINEERING WAS OF A HIGH LEVEL, AND EQUALLY AMAZING WAS THEIR SKILL IN CUTTING HARD STONE LIKE GRANITE AND QUARTZ WITH SUCH PRECISION. THEY WERE ALSO CLOSELY LINKED TO ASTRONOMY: AUTHORITATIVE HYPOTHESES REVEAL THE USE OF THIS SITE AS AN OBSERVATORY. FOR EXAMPLE, THE INTIHUATANA STONE WAS USED TO PINPOINT THE MOMENTS OF THE EQUINOXES BY MEANS OF A PRINCIPLE SIMILAR TO THAT OF THE MERIDIAN. YET THE STONE'S MOST FASCINAT-ING FUNCTION WAS TO CONNECT THE WORLD OF HUMANS WITH THE HEREAFTER; ONE MERELY HAD TO LAY HIS HEAD ON THE ROCK TO BEGIN A MYSTICAL JOURNEY OF SPIRITUALISTIC AND SPIRITUAL VISIONS.

Obviously, these doubts, plus the lack of any form of writing to help us to clarify them, have given rise to all sorts of suppositions, even including the idea that tops them all and solves every problem: Who could realize such marvelous feats of engineering and architecture but a band of aliens from outer space on an outing? This explanation would help us to dispel all doubts, but oddly has not been taken seriously by archeologists and historians. For that matter, in this portion of the world that was once sacred, then faded into oblivion, and is now being invaded by tourism, there is room for all types of interpretation.

According to a local myth, in the beginning there was only darkness and chaos, after which the creator god generated the stars, the moon, and the sun, and the sun god Inti chose the Incas as his children to transform disorder into order on Earth. This justified the Incas' thirst for dominion, understood as a mission on behalf of their god, but it may also be a valid explanation for their being able to erect a city that blended so well into the natural elements as to become an integral part of them, in a relationship that should serve as an example to us.

LICANCABUR

Altitude: 19,423 ft. (5920 m) a.s.l.
Prominence: 4678 ft. (1426 m)
Topographic isolation: not available
Coordinates: latitude 22°50'0" S; longitude 67°52'58" W
Location: San Pedro de Atacama

A SEGMENT OF MARS

For the inhabitants of the Atacama area, this is the Mountain of the People, a subduction volcano of the Holocene epoch, which has given no signs of recent activity. To be more precise, it is a stratovolcano: its rather viscous lava tended to solidify before moving too far from the crater and thus created a steep and compact conical shape. The peak is in Chile and is occupied by a crater lake 295 x 230 ft. (90 x 70 m) with a maximum depth of 26 ft. (8 m). This body of water freezes over during the cold season, and the weather conditions are particularly hostile to life, so much so that scientists have found interesting parameters to study the features of Mars, which are considered similar. Despite its not-so-prompt hospitality, the mountain enraptures those who climb it, above all thanks to the panoramic view, which ranges from the Laguna Verde to the Salar de Atacama. The great number of Inca finds up to the top of Licancabur demonstrates that humans lived here at least as far back as 500 years ago, and it also proves the absence of major eruptions in the following period. It may be that due to such long-term frequentation, the news of the first successful ascent in modern times—ostensibly to be attributed to the local farmer Severo Titichoca—was not accompanied by fascinating accounts of the feat, the only exception being the fact that it inaugurated a tendency to steal archaeological artifacts indiscriminately. But we know very little about this, since these events took place in 1884 and are scarcely documented.

THE SURROUNDINGS OF MARS

~

Licancabur is in symbiosis with its surroundings. Toward Bolivia, it keeps an eye on the Laguna Verde, which, although at the foot of the former, also lies at a notable altitude—14,190 ft. (4325 m) above sea level. The color of this salt flat is conditioned by the abundance of copper, magnesium, and arsenic. Their sediment reacts in different ways, depending on the winds that ripple the water, taking on variable tones from blue to turquoise and emerald green. On the Chilean side is a highland with absolutely unique features, the Atacama Desert. This is one of the most arid zones on Earth, thanks to the ideal combination of dry air, altitude, and a total lack of light pollution, and it is perfect for the observation of the stars. With an irregular rhythm, from five up to seven years, a spectacular phenomenon occurs in this desert, when the landscape is filled with blossoms and becomes a magical expanse of pink and yellow.

SIBLING RIVALRY

✺

LICANCABUR AND LASCÁR WERE BROTHERS, BUT NOT TYPI-
CAL ONES. THEY WERE HANDSOME, HEALTHY, AND ROBUST
VOLCANOES, AND UP TO A CERTAIN POINT GOT ALONG
FAIRLY WELL, WHICH IS TO SAY THAT THERE WERE NO PROB-
LEMS OF ENVY, COMPETITION, OR INHERITANCE BETWEEN
THE TWO. HOWEVER, THIS HARMONIOUS UNION TURNED
OUT TO BE COUNTERPRODUCTIVE THE MOMENT THE TWO,
WHOSE TASTES WERE TOO SIMILAR, FELL IN LOVE WITH THE
SAME WOMAN, PRINCESS JURIQUES. SHE PLAYED A WAITING
GAME FOR A BIT BEFORE LETTING HERSELF BE SEDUCED BY
LICANCABUR—A LEGITIMATE CHOICE, BUT ONE THAT LASCÁR
SIMPLY COULD NOT ACCEPT AT ALL. INCONSOLABLE, HE WEPT
FOR MONTHS AND MONTHS, SO MUCH SO THAT THIS CREAT-
ED A HUGE SALT LAKE IN A BASIN. THEN ONE FINE DAY, HIS
SADNESS DISAPPEARED, AND LASCÁR FOUND THE STRENGTH
TO REACT . . . BUT BADLY.

No sooner did he feel new energy flowing in his body than his depression became rage and he flew into a passion, spewing fire high and low. This hormonal, high-calorie reaction immediately caused the pleasant body of water to drain, thus transforming it into the Atacama Desert. But the most pitiful aspect was that one of the deadly projectiles hit—by chance?—poor Juriques, killing her instantly in the typical style of the worst macho violence. At this point, it was Licancabur who sank into abysmal sadness, but he at least kept his self-control for an indefinite period without triggering hydrogeological instability. After an interminable period, he managed to deal with his grief and fell hopelessly in love with Kimal, a foreign princess who for some time had spent her days observing him. That's how Licancabur was: he liked princesses. However, evidently this was not to be. A bureaucratic technicality immediately cropped up: that is to say, marriage between persons of different nationalities was forbidden, and would be so forever. So Kimal got to work and prayed as hard as she could to change this regrettable situation. She insisted so much with her pleas that the gods—who had probably lost their patience—allowed the two lovers to meet once a year, during the December 21 solstice. Indeed, on that day, the longest of the year in the Southern Hemisphere, the shadows of Cerro Kimal and Licancabur overlap partially, celebrating their love. In other versions, Lascár is the father, Juriques the brother, and Kimal the contested woman, while Licancabur is not exactly what you would call a saint. The only certainty is that the volcano Juriques was struck and lacerated, as its chipped shape demonstrates. For that matter, it is a well-known fact that when they get down to business, volcanoes can be rather aggressive.

CERRO TORRE

Altitude: 10,252 ft. (3128 m) a.s.l.
Prominence: 4026 ft. (1227 m)
Topographic isolation: not available
Coordinates: latitude 49°17'26" S; longitude 73°05'56" W
Location: Santa Cruz province

UNCONQUERABLE

Patagonia: at the Chilean and Argentinian border. Cerro Torre, the tallest peak in a range with three other peaks (Torre Egger, Punta Herron, and Cerro Standhardt), leaves you speechless: you could thumb through a thesaurus as much as you wanted, but would never find the appropriate words. Reality sometimes transcends human expression, and we can only bow in submission like a humble knight in the presence of his sovereign.

Slim, pointed, virtually unconquerable with its smooth faces—like sheets of paper with imprinted, indelible memories—this mountain 10,252 ft. (3128 m) high lies at the edge of a continental glacier, covering an area of 8077 sq. mi. (13,000 sq. km). Before reaching the summit, one must first go up a granite face 2953 ft. (900 m) high, and then some. Although vertical, the rock is a firm and safe foothold compared to the treacherous rime ice mushroom that covers the last 55 yards (50 m), and the peak is battered by the Patagonian wind and subject to unpredictable and ruthless weather. So why climb it? This is a question with no possible answer for anyone immune to the demon of the descent who trembles at the mere thought that a clumsy, heavy creature—without wings—could wish to be up there. At the same time, the question makes no sense if this demon is part of your makeup: the existence alone of that peak is an attraction stronger than fear or prudence.

SCREAM OF STONE

~

The "Cerro Torre affair" has filled page after page, and will continue to do so, because rock, although it does not forget, is not able to narrate, and the truth remains suspended in the fog of our imagination. This is the huge contradiction of mountaineers: they are generous, almost heroes, ready to risk their lives for themselves and others, humble persons devoted to nature—yet eager to demonstrate the indemonstrable, challenge the sky, death, and even God, if they are believers. Outstanding yet wild men, united and sympathetic in misfortune but capable of inveighing against one another and, blinded by ambition, of lying in order to be the first on a peak. In short, a mountaineer is a human.

Cerro Torre is the ideal theater for a competition with an uncertain ending, not so much because of the altitude as for its shape and the unreliable weather conditions, which do not offer any certainty regarding the duration of the climb.

In the beginning was Father Alberto Maria de Agostini, a missionary from the Piedmont region of Italy who for over 40 years (1910 to the late 1950s) devoted himself to the study and exploration of South America. He was also a mountaineer, cartographer, author, cinematographer, and you name it, and it was he who made Cerro Torre popular in Italy. In the second half of the 1950s, mountaineers were at fever pitch. After various skirmishes, approaches, and climbs that failed aborning—such as those of the almost-contemporary Bonatti-Mauri and Maestri-Detassis duos—in January 1959 the Maestri, Egger, and Fava expedition took the lead, discouraging others who were still organizing their ascent. Difficulties due to bad weather arose in the first days, which were spent setting up gear on the initial pitch. On January 28, the first two set off to conquer the summit, while Fava returned to the base camp to wait for them. On January 31, they seemed to have achieved their goal but, according to Maestri's account, there was no cause for celebration because of the unbearable angst they felt due to the huge risks entailed in the descent. This premonition of disaster became reality on February 2 when, while setting up the last bivouac on a face, the two were overwhelmed by an avalanche of snow and ice. Egger disappeared and Maestri, having passed the night there, somehow managed the descent they would have to make. Cesare Fava found Maestri, who was injured and trembling, shocked by the death of his friend. His confusing account was soon doubted and confuted, and the discovery of some of Egger's gear retrieved five years later came to nothing: there was no trace of the camera, the only possible proof that they had reached the summit.

Ten years later, Maestri returned but tried another route. The ascent is famous because of the 220-pound (100 kg) compressor he used to drill with bolts a 984-foot (300 m) rock face—and then left hanging there. It was an extremely long trek that did not reach the ice mushroom on the peak because, according to Maestri, it was not part of the mountain. Not even this second climb helped to dispel the doubts, and in fact the first officially acknowledged ascent was made by the Lecco Spiders (Ragni di Lecco) in 1974. The famous mountaineer Reinhold Messner wrote a book, Scream of Stone, about this dispute after writing a screenplay for the film of the same name directed by Werner Herzog.

BROTHERS IN ARMS

∾

THE YEAR 2022 WITNESSED ANOTHER ILL-FATED CLIMB, A COMBINATION OF COURAGE AND SORROW. ANOTHER SPIDER TEAM—MATTEO DELLA BORDELLA, DAVID BACCI, AND MATTEO DE ZAIACOMO—HAD JUST OPENED A NEW ROUTE. ON THE SUMMIT THEY MET TOMÁS AGUILÓ AND CORRADO PESCE, WHO HAD ALSO DONE THE SAME.

After a brief and intense moment of sharing the joy of conquest, Korra and Tomy (their nicknames) descended the north face at night, while the Spiders bivouacked on the summit. The next day, after an extenuating descent that began on the renowned Compressor Route, the three friends learned that at dawn Korra and Tomy had been hit and injured by a powerful avalanche of stones and ice. There was no way out: they had to go back up the face to rescue their colleagues. They found Tomás, who had managed to cover part of the route despite atrocious suffering, and put him in a safe place, while nothing could be done to help Korra. The new route marked out by the Lecco Spiders is called *Brothers in Arms*, in honor of those who have lost their lives on mountains, both here and elsewhere.

KIRKJUFELL

Altitude: 1519 ft. (463 m) a.s.l.
Prominence: 1473 ft. (449 m)
Topographic isolation: not available
Coordinates: latitude 64°56'51" N; longitude 23°18'39" W
Location: Grundarfjörður

ARROWHEAD

Technically, being only 1519 feet (463 m) above sea level, the "Church Mountain" is not even a mountain, yet it is one of the most fascinating sites in Iceland, and not only there. Its shape, at once barren and pleasant, reminds some people of a bell tower, while others see it as an arrowhead or rose thorn. Again, it could be regarded as the visible part of a partially hidden creature, such as a shark's dorsal fin or the crest on a dinosaur's back. Its stark elegance, which is occasionally mirrored in the small lake at its foot, has a constant and playful relationship with the surrounding natural elements, as if that peak were the focal point of the variable sky and sea, allowing them to revolve around it without losing their way or running off. This basaltic massif of volcanic origin—which is not a volcano, but consists of layers of lavas dating to various eras, and thus of great geological interest—acquired its present shape when glaciers eroded its walls by means of flow.

According to Inuit terminology, in the past the mountain may have been called Nunatak, a sort of rock island smack in the middle of a sea of ice, a reference point and often the cradle of vegetation that is unique because of its isolation from the rest of the world. While not presenting great difficulty, the ascent to the summit requires crossing over steep and turfy slopes that are very exposed, with sections that can become hazardous, especially when it rains or when they are covered with ice.

TO EVERY PEAK
ITS OWN SKY

~

The relationship between a mountain and its sky
is always crucial, but in this case it is even more
so, because it is a sky both spacious and nearby.
Above all, here we are speaking of a firmament
brimming with mystery, with its extreme seasonal
changes and one of the most amazing phenomena one
could ever observe, supernatural more than natural: the Northern Lights. Basically this consists
of an interaction of charged particles from the
Sun with others in the atmosphere, together with
the action of the terrestrial magnetic field. The
result is simply staggering and cannot but make
one think of magic, somewhere between dreams and
apprehension. It is so beautiful with its dramatic, vivid fluorescent appearance, so scintillat-
ing, that it seems almost artificial, so glittery
that it makes one think of kitsch. Fortunately,
the sharp profile of Kirkjufell reassures us,
reminding us that it is all real. The best period
to enjoy the spectacle of the Northern Lights is
from October to March, while the phenomenon may
also occur out of season.

FANTASY
AND POETIC THEORIES

∾

SO REAL AS TO SEEM INVENTED, THESE SUBLIME AND WILD PLACES HAVE BEEN THE IDEAL SETTING FOR MANY SCENES OF THE SIXTH AND SEVENTH SEASONS OF *GAME OF SWORDS*. HERE WE SEE JON SNOW WANDERING ABOUT THE REMOTE LAND NORTH OF THE WALL TOGETHER WITH HIS FELLOW NORTHMEN, THE FREE PEOPLE WHO REFUSE TO GIVE IN. THE ARROWHEAD MOUNTAIN APPEARS BOTH IN ITS WINTER GARB AND WEARING ITS GREEN ATTIRE AT TWO DIFFERENT MOMENTS. IN THIS CASE, FICTION AND REALITY ARE CLOSELY LINKED IN THE MOST CLASSICAL MANNER, BECAUSE THE LOVE STORY BETWEEN JON AND YGRITTE LEFT THE SCREENPLAY AND BECAME A REAL MARRIAGE BETWEEN THE TWO ACTORS.

For that matter, this land of contrasts, where the cold is in such close contact with the inflammable elements that emerge from the subsoil, has for some time been famous and almost emblematic for its harshness.

The great poet Giacomo Leopardi, who in fact never set foot on Iceland, describes it as a particularly harsh and inhospitable place. The extremely long cold winters and the scorching heat of the summers, the violence of the storms and the threatening roar of the Hecla volcano, the fires and earthquakes— do not leave the Icelander in peace, nor are the countermeasures free from troublesome side effects such as the fires necessary for heating that dry the throat and skin and therefore become a constant disturbance. This stratospheric manifestation of power demonstrates how tiny and insignificant we are in the presence of nature.

MONT BLANC

Altitude: 14,692 ft. (4478 m) a.s.l.
Prominence: 15,407 ft. (4696 m)
Topographic isolation: 1747 mi. (2812 km)
Coordinates: latitude 45°49'58" N; longitude 6°51'52.88" E
Location: Courmayeur, Chamonix

THE KING OF THE ALPS

The highest peak in the Alps and in all Europe was formed about 300 million years ago in the depths of the earth, when a gigantic magma bubble solidified and was transformed into granite. This immense block was then pushed upward by the fold in the Alpine Arc and rose up thanks to the erosion of the upper sediments. Its altitude is monitored continuously because of the changes in the layer of ice that covers the summit. Robust, wide, surrounded by 65 glaciers and by other mountains, Mont Blanc is not distinguished for its pointed peak shooting up to the firmament, but rather sits sedately like an old and wise warrior who doesn't need to show his muscles. More than a mountain, it is a world, and as such bears infinite parallel entities within and on itself. Besides being a dessert and a brand, Mont Blanc separates Italy and France while at the same time linking them via a tunnel almost 7 miles (11 km) long; it is crossed by cableways, furrowed by abandoned mines, and not only has the usual mountain refuges but also hosts important laboratories run by the Institute of Physics of Interplanetary Space of Turin. It has inspired poets—especially Englishmen, unfamiliar with mountains, on the Grand Tour—and has contributed to the creation of the mountaineering story genre. In a tragic and sublime example of things gone haywire that is almost superfluous to underscore, Mont Blanc has been the theater of heartbreaking events such as episodes of war, serious airplane accidents, the terrible tunnel fire that cost 39 lives, and naturally the continuous tribute of blood required by mountaineering (it is estimated that more than 6000 persons have died over the years).

THE JOY AND SORROW OF CONQUEST

~

The same bittersweet cloud envelops the account of the first official ascent of Mont Blanc. The collector of crystals Balmat and the physician Paccard were the first to set foot on the summit, after a climb of almost 15 hours. It was late afternoon on 8 August 1786 according to the precious diary kept by the Prussian Baron Von Gersdorff, who was observing them with binoculars from a ledge above Chamonix. Less than half an hour later, the two departed, reaching the French town after spending the night bivouacking. At Chamonix, Balmat learned of the death of his newborn daughter, which had occurred the day before, while he was finishing the ascent.

The following year, the Genevan scientist De Saussure, an enthusiastic supporter and sponsor of the feat, decided to make the climb as well and did so with Balmat and a super team of 18 guides who carried provisions, scientific instruments, and, it seems, even a camp bed. For quite some time, due to jealousy and mystification, this second ascent usurped the first one, deleting Paccard's name from the account. The physician obtained posthumous justice only in the early 20th century, when Barone Von Gersdorff's famous diary cropped up.

FRENEY

∾

THIS IS A STORY OF TRAGIC AND HYPNOTIC FASCINATION THAT YOU COULD READ A HUNDRED TIMES, HOPING FOR A HAPPIER ENDING THAT NEVER ARRIVES. IN 1961, COURMAYEUR WAS TOTALLY DIFFERENT FROM THE CHIC SKIING LOCALE WE KNOW TODAY, A SPARTAN OUTPOST LOVED BY TRUE AFICIONADOS OF THE MOUNTAIN PER SE. FOR YEARS, WALTER BONATTI HAD DREAMT OF OPENING A ROUTE ON THE CENTRAL PILLAR OF THE FREINEY GLACIER TO THE SUMMIT, AND IT APPEARED THE RIGHT MOMENT HAD ARRIVED. ON THE STAR-FILLED NIGHT OF JULY 10 AT THE FOURCHE BIVOUAC, BONATTI, WITH HIS TWO FRIENDS OGGIONI AND GALLIENI, DECIDED TO ROPE-CLIMB TOGETHER WITH FOUR FRENCH MOUNTAINEERS LED BY PIERRE MAZEAUD, WHO HAD HAD THE SAME IDEA.

Everything went smoothly, thanks to the good weather and the seven climbers' enthusiasm and skill. At this point, a simple alteration on the part of destiny could have transformed this account into one episode in a thousand, memorable only for those who experienced it, recorded in some dusty almanac. True, because they were only a few dozen yards from the end of the face and it was only early afternoon, when the weather suddenly decided to turn its back on the seven climbers, who were forced to retreat as quickly as possible to the two ledges above Chandelle, the only crevices that could offer them shelter, albeit fragile. Then the sky seemed determined to assail the small group that had dared to defy it. The magnetic force of the lightning, attracted by the pegs and axes, struck them from close by, especially Pierre Kohlmann, short-circuiting his hearing aid. After the rain came the snow, which at that altitude has no season. The two leaders agreed it was best to wait for a letup that would allow them to gain the summit in a hurry; then the others could reach them, after which they would all descend on easier routes rather than face a very long, dangerous, and depressing descent on the pillar. After two interminable nights on the face, this seemed to be the logical solution to their dilemma, but it was merely an illusion. Just as

Bonatti and Mazeaud were getting ready to leave, the weather worsened again. On the third night of the bivouac, they were at the end of their tether, as were their nerves: now the only way to save their lives was to return to the base, which would take a whole day. But their relief was short-lived, because it was impossible for the rescuers to find them, and they were forced to reach the Gamba via an extremely long and risky route, with the snow up to their necks. Vieille had stopped, giving in to the cold and fatigue; Guillaume ended up falling into a crevasse; and Oggioni had lost all hope and no longer moved. The group was now like a wounded pachyderm: they had to separate to seek help. The last trick of destiny offered a sample of the most delusional forms of the human psyche, which occurred a few steps from their arrival. Kohlmann, who was totally isolated due to his deafness, had somehow resisted but went berserk; he saw Gallieni put his hand in his pocket and, thinking he was about to take out a pistol, attacked him with all his remaining energy. Bonatti and Gallieni managed to subdue him and take him to the hut, totally exhausted and just in time to hand him over to the rescuers, but the Frenchman died of exposure. Of the French team, only Mazeaud managed to survive. Mont Blanc is there, a silent witness of both tragedy and glory. I read the ending of the story once again, but it is the same.

MATTERHORN

Altitude: 14,692 ft. (4478 m) a.s.l.
Prominence: 1383 ft. (1031 m)
Topographic isolation: 8.5 mi. (13.7 km)
Coordinates: latitude 45°58'35" N; longitude 7°39'30" E
Location: Breuil-Cervinia, Zermatt

THE VERY ESSENCE OF A MOUNTAIN

Many children see the pointed shape of the Matterhorn for the first time on the magical containers of the famous Caran d'Ache colored pencils. With its majestic perfection, this peak dominates the underlying landscape, the herdsman's huts with stone roofs and blossoming rhododendrons in the shade of the Swiss flag. Everything begins with childhood. Then one day you discover that that mountain really exists, and it is somewhat like seeing New York for the first time: you feel quite at home because you have already seen the details of the city in books and movies.

The Matterhorn is a cross between a wolf's tooth and a pyramid, and is so distinct in its isolation that its magnetism is felt even at a great distance. Indeed, what is a rather obvious phenomenon when seen from the surrounding valleys becomes even more prominent when observed from afar: for long moments we end up enchanted, struck, slaves forced to bow down in the presence of such esthetic power.

It is not surprising that the history of the venerable granite peak began 90 million years ago due to the collision of the African and European tectonic plates. In an almost inconceivable lapse of time, the combination of movements of the Earth's crust and the erosive action of glaciation and of relentless atmospheric agents created the shape we now see, our eyes glued to those craggy rock faces spotted with snow.

THE COSTLY CONQUEST (1865)

~

For a long period, the summit (a combination of "meadows" and "peak" in German) remained unvanquished, becoming a challenge, and almost an obsession, for many mountaineers. The final competition took place between Edward Whymper and the Italian Jean-Antoine Carrel from the Aosta Valley, two friends and rivals who had already attempted the ascent together and failed. In the end, it was the Englishman who first planted his flag on 14 July 1865, after opening a route on the Swiss slope, arriving before his rival, who led an expedition from the Italian side. However, the mountain demanded a heavy tribute that is known as the greatest tragedy in mountaineering: during the descent, one of the seven persons in the rope team, the young Hadow, slipped and dragged three other companions with him in a fatal fall of more than 1000 meters. Nowadays, thousands of climbers reach the summit every summer. Nevertheless, the ascent is still difficult and has cost the lives of more than 500 persons.

THE LAST EXPLOIT
(1965)

∾

CLOSELY CONNECTED TO THE FIRST CONQUEST OF THE MATTERHORN IS THE MOST INSANE FEAT EVER ACHIEVED IN THIS AREA, NARRATED BY THE PROTAGONIST HIMSELF IN PAGES THAT GIVE YOU CHILLS AND GOOSEBUMPS. IT WAS PRECISELY 100 YEARS AFTER WHYMPER'S ACHIEVEMENT WHEN WALTER BONATTI DECIDED TO SAY FAREWELL TO THE WORLD OF EXTREME MOUNTAINEERING WITH ONE LAST GREAT ASCENT THAT WAS VIRTUALLY IMPOSSIBLE. HE CHALLENGED THE NORTH FACE OF THE MATTERHORN, IN WINTER AND ALONE, OPENING A NEW ROUTE OF EXCEPTIONAL DIFFICULTY, SPENDING FOUR NIGHTS ON THE FACE WITH OUTDATED GEAR AND TRADITIONAL METHODS, INDULGING IN THIS FINAL PARENTHESIS OF SPLENDOR.

That sense of sublime isolation, of wrenching yet marvelous solitude, conveys the idea of what peaks are, what they can represent for those who have been there as well as those who only observe them with due and humble respect. The arrival of this superhuman man on the summit—where the guides who had come via other routes put the cross blown down by the wind back on its feet in his honor—contains so much of the fascinating history of mountaineering that, like the perfect materialization of a metaphor, it includes in the same circle the trajectory of spotless heroes and the baseness of envy, lies, and jealousy that all too often spoil human enterprises. Up there, Bonatti took his leave from that type of spasmodic competition and undertook another difficult mission: to tell the story of mountains, emphasizing the epic aspects—and above all the spiritual implications—of that wild, harsh, and solitary world.

THE CIME DI LAVAREDO

Altitude: 9839 ft. (2999 m) a.s.l.
Prominence: 1863 ft. (568 m)
Topographic isolation: not available
Coordinates: latitude 46°37'06" N; longitude 12°18'19" E
Location: Auronzo/Dobbiaco

THREE FINGERS AGAINST THE SKY

Somebody please find one! There must be an architect, an artist, or a genius who has imagined all this. It can't be a coincidence, a nasty story about faults, folds, and erosion. No. That would mean we haven't understood anything. We always say we want to change the world, but what precisely is there to change? Certainly not the three peaks of Lavaredo, the symbol of the Dolomites, because they are perfect just as Mother Nature made them. These three rock obelisks, distinct but near one another, are known as Cima Ovest (Western Peak), 9754 ft. (2973 m) above sea level; the middle Cima Grande (Big Peak), 9839 ft. (2999 m); and the eastern Cima Piccola (Little Peak), 9373 ft. (2857 m). They were created by the erosion of the layer of dolomite that once occupied the entire zone. The formation of the Dolomites is quite articulated and particularly interesting from a geological standpoint: most of the rock that constitutes the stratigraphy dates to at least 250 million years ago, from the late Paleozoic to the late Mesozoic. Moreover, the processes of deformation, erosion, and slip are still in progress. These factors, together with the association between volcanic and dolomitic rocks, make this region unique in the world. The plateau lying at the foot of the three fingers pointing to the sky, with a play of light that makes them change in an infinite number of indescribable nuances, is a watershed in the literal sense of the term: there are torrents that one day will merge with the Danube and streams that will join the Adige and Piave rivers.

A BEACON IN THE NIGHT

~

The crest that includes the three peaks is now the dividing line between the provinces of Bolzano and Belluno with the respective towns of Dobbiaco and Auronzo, and it has been the natural border between Austrian and Italian regions since the Middle Ages. This position proved to be crucial when Italy entered World War One. For three years, the area was the theater of terrifying clashes with alternating fortune: sad and heroic days that the stone cannot narrate. In the summer of 1915, after three weeks of hard labor, three groups of soldiers placed a large lighthouse—and a cannon—on the Cima Grande to illuminate and confound the enemy from a high position. This object, which weighed about 1322 pounds, was disassembled and then reassembled on the peak, which was lowered by means of explosives in order to leave more room for the light to pass through.

Changing the subject to something lighter yet veined with heroism, the three peaks were often the privileged spectators of the conclusion of epic stages of the Giro d'Italia bicycle race. In truth, the peaks did not always observe the race. For example, the arrival in 2013 was almost something that had to be imagined, with the sky so low that it reduced the view to a thread, and a blizzard that spread snow everywhere and whitened the cyclists' eyelids. The race leader Vincenzo Nibali arrived at the finish line with his arms upraised, his pink jersey standing out in the fog and amidst that uncontrolled excitement that accompanies the historic exploits of sport.

This same setting had already played host to the challenge between Felice Gimondi and Eddy Merckx in 1967 and 1968. In the first case, the Italian won, but the stage was annulled because too many cyclists were given pushes during the climb; while in the second it was the Belgian who triumphed.

Obviously, the three peaks are also a sort of terrestrial paradise (projected toward the sky) for mountaineering aficionados. Three peaks, three first conquests, all on the south slope, in the period from 1869 to 1881. Paul Grohmann, with the guides Franz Innerkofler and Peter Salcher, conquered the Cima Grande with a perfectly organized ascent that took only three hours. Ten years later, it was the turn of the Cima Occidentale; and in 1881 the Cima Piccola, long considered unconquerable because of the great difficulties involved, was ascended. With time, many other routes were opened; the most challenging one was the long winter climb up the north face, which many regarded as an insane undertaking.

THE ROOSTER AND THE GIANT

∾

IT IS SAID THAT AT THE ROOT OF THESE MOUNTAINS WAS A STUBBORN AND UNREQUITED LOVE. THE PRINCESS VAL D'AN-SIEI WAS BEAUTIFUL, AND ONE OF HER MANY VIRTUES WAS A MELODIOUS VOICE. THE AIR VIBRATED WITH HER SINGING THROUGH ALL THE MOUNTAINS, AND THE GIANT LAVAREDO FELL HOPELESSLY IN LOVE WITH THIS MAIDEN. BUT SHE WANT-ED NOTHING TO DO WITH HIM AND GRANTED HER FAVORS TO ANOTHER—AND ORDINARY—GIANT, THE CLASSIC GOOD-FOR-NOTHING LOUT WHO ATTRACTS INGENUOUS GIRLS AS A MAGNET ATTRACTS METAL.

And, as was to be expected, the ne'er-do-well abandoned her shortly afterward, leaving her with a baby boy named Auronzo. The good Lavaredo, whose pure love was never susceptible to anger, cut three huge spires in the rock with his own hands and gave them to his beloved and her child to comfort them in their sad lot.

There is another entertaining story connected to these peaks, a tale of parochialism and the struggle for survival. The pastureland was scarce; consequently, the rivalry between the inhabitants of Dobbiaco and Auronzo was becoming intolerable. It was established that two women, one from each town, would solve this problem under the careful scrutiny of two witnesses from the opposing faction. They were to leave their respective homes at dawn with a stone in their hands, and the point where they met would become the border between the two territories. The woman from Auronzo, who was more cunning, poked the local rooster with her knitting needles, making it crow earlier than usual. So she took off well before dawn with the two notaries at her heels, winning a portion of land for her town much larger than the one that remained for its rivals. This is why its citizens have a certain fondness for roosters.

KILIMANJARO

Altitude: 19,341 ft. (5895 m) a.s.l.
Prominence: 19,308 ft. (5885 m)
Topographic isolation: 3424 miles (5510 km)
Coordinates: latitude 3°04'33" S; longitude 37°21'12" E
Location: the border between northeast Tanzania and Kenya

SNOW ON THE EQUATOR

Mt. Kilimanjaro contains many worlds, and observing it from below your eyes can range over the savannah and the snow, caressing every nuance, with the thin clouds serving as counterpoint. Indisputably the highest peak in Africa, it is a stratovolcano formed by three principal craters, the extinct Shira and Mawenzi, and between them Kibo, which is a bit irritable (dormant), although there is no certain proof concerning its latest eruption, which probably occurred about two centuries ago. Kilimanjaro was formed on the edge of a divergent boundary, the type of movement that can make the magma from the lowest strata on our planet emerge. While a conspicuous amount of lava has been seen inside the mountain at a depth of 1312 ft. (400 m), on the outside of the summit is the Rebmann glacier, which, however, retreated in the last century—and, should it continue to do so, will not last for long. The pluvial forest at its foot offers refuge to such animals as leopards, antelopes, buffaloes, baboons, and guengon monkeys. The climb up the Marangu route is neither risky nor difficult, but it must be taken with local guides and porters and entails a five-day walk, as well as physical fitness, given the high altitude.

The wide area around the massif—almost 656 square miles (1700 sq. km)—is protected by a large national park and consists of four distinct climatic belts. Below 9186 ft. (2800 m) there are impressive trees with long trunks typical of a pluvial forest; up to 13,123 ft. (4000 m) is a heath of shrubs; a high-altitude desert lies from 13,123 to 16,404 ft. (5000 m); and above this is a landscape of stones, ice, and snow. This is a unique patrimony of virgin flora and fauna that was duly acknowledged by UNESCO in 1987.

ON THE ROOF OF AFRICA

~

This mountain, whose size is made even more evident by the vast surrounding plain, was mentioned in some ancient accounts. Ptolemy wrote of a snow-covered mountain in the lands of barbarous cannibals. It was concretely "discovered" by Europeans in 1848, when the German explorer and missionary Rebmann managed to observe it close up and confirm the surprising presence of snow in the equatorial zone.

However, the conquest had to wait until 1889, with the expedition of Hans Meyer and the mountaineer Ludwig Purtscheller. Meyer had already made two attempts. In the first, he had had to give up due to mountain sickness and the sheer fatigue of the ascent; while in the second an Arab sheik had a hand in it by kidnapping him during a local revolt and then letting him free in exchange for a ransom. Stubborn, and having learned from these experiences, Meyer adopted a more gradual, prudent approach, setting up one base at the foot of the mountain and another at an altitude of 14,108 ft. (4300 m). The day of the ascent, the two set off in the middle of the night in order to reach the glacier early in the morning. From that point, the climb became arduous, first due to the prohibitive slopes and then because the snow was waist-deep.

Exhausted, the two men returned to the glacier base despite having arrived less than 218 feet (200 m) from the top. The plan was to rest for two days and then resume the climb, taking advantage of the footprints they had left and their familiarity with the route. This strategy proved to be perfect, and on the morning of October 6 the German flag was planted on the roof of Africa, an apocalyptic setting of black rock resting on a sea of clouds.

AT THE HOUSE OF GOD

∾

ACCORDING TO THE MASAI, MT. KILIMANJARO IS THE HOUSE OF GOD, AND ONLY THOSE WITH GOOD THOUGHTS AND A PURE HEART CAN APPROACH IT. AN ANCIENT MASAI FABLE CONCERNS A LEOPARD THAT FOR THREE DAYS CHASED A GAZELLE, WHICH SOUGHT REFUGE FROM THE GOD NGAI, WHOSE THRONE WAS RIGHT ON THE SUMMIT OF THE VOLCANO. OBVIOUSLY, NGAI OFFERED THE FRIGHTENED ANIMAL HIS SUPPORT, WHILE THE LEOPARD, WHICH ACTED PURELY OUT OF THE NOT-SO-NOBLE INSTINCT OF HUNGER, WAS DOOMED TO DIE OF COLD IN THE SNOW.

In one of his short stories, *The Snows of Kilimanjaro*, Ernest Hemingway also used the same image when the protagonist Harry dreams of flying to the top of the great mountain: "Close to the western summit there is the dried and frozen carcass of a leopard. No one has explained what the leopard was seeking at that altitude." In any case, it seems that a pair of frozen leopards really were found in that zone, and the explanation must lie in the sinister stories of chases among wild animals, while the most debated point is that of divine intervention, which is left to one's individual conscience, as always.

Another pleasant but much less spiritual story is connected to Queen Victoria. It was said that in 1890, when marking the border between the two colonies that fortunately became Kenya and Tanzania, the sovereign insisted on giving the mountain to her beloved nephew, the Kaiser Wilhelm II. And we say that today's children are spoiled!

TABLE MOUNTAIN

Altitude: 3563 ft. (1086 m) a.s.l.
Prominence: 3461 ft. (1055 m)
Topographic isolation: not available
Coordinates: latitude 33°57'00" S; longitude 18°24'59.98" E
Location: Cape Town, Western Cape province

THE MOUNTAIN IN THE CITY

Mountains are like people: you will never find two that are equal. Yes, they are all different, but some are more different than others. First of all, Table Mountain is part of that group of atypical mountains without a summit, without the classic pointed peak that our childhood legacy has taught us to attribute to any self-respecting mountain—with the sole authorized exception of volcanoes. Table Mountain, on the other hand, resembles the top of a table and is not ashamed and makes no secret of it. On the contrary, the very name declares it explicitly. Again, in general, mountains tend to be remote, haughty, wild, and unconquerable, thus stimulating Man's thirst for adventure. But not Table Mountain. It lies there without fear or snobbery, comfortably on the shoulders of Cape Town, to such a degree that it is an integral part of its skyline as if it were just another skyscraper—and it doesn't even scrape that much, given its shape. For that matter, there is the saying that if Mu-

hammad does not go to the mountain, the latter will go to Muhammad. In this case, there it is among us, integrated and accessible both via paths and the cableway inaugurated in 1929. The lower part of Table Mountain consists of granite and metamorphic rock, while the upper half is made up of horizontal beds of Paleozoic sandstone that rise up 3563 feet (1086 m) above sea level. It owes its name to its silhouette, steep on the sides and horizontal at the top, which forms a scenic balcony in a one-to-one relationship with the urban area and the ocean, a site that overlooks everything and that can be seen from everywhere. The lower slopes are inhabited by coniferous woods, surprising vegetation including orchids and various species of protea, and vineyards and villas. The upper section is more austere, and the view of the city, the hills, and the entire Cape peninsula is simply breathtaking. At the north end of the range are the Devil's Peak and the Lion's Head, with its paw.

ONE DEVIL OF A WIND

~

Arriving from the east is the Cape Doctor, a gusty and recurrent wind from the sea that batters the sky of the city and clashes with Table Mountain, creating the cloud of humidity that often covers the mesa like a white tablecloth. Such places cannot but give rise to all types of legends, as is proper. When the Dutch pirate Van Hunks landed here, he loved to climb up the Table and smoke his pipe while leaning against his favorite tree and gazing at the ocean below. One day, he found that his place had been taken by someone he had never seen—a foreigner, perhaps?—who was a tad insolent and wouldn't hear of moving off, not even after the Dutchman's lively protests. In fact, he even claimed that that tiny plot of land was his. What ensued was a duel with gusts of smoke, resulting in two huge clouds that soon merged in their struggle for dominion. In the end, the aspiring usurper was defeated, overpowered by coughing fits, the last one of which made him bend his head forward, revealing a nice pair of horns that had not been visible up till then. In conclusion, that piece of work was none other than the Devil in person, whom the dauntless Van Hunks had just defeated. But, as we all know, the devil is by no means a polite gentleman who accepts rules easily, so the duel resumes continuously and the area tends to almost always be rather cloudy. For that matter, it seems that Hendrick Van Der Decken, the captain of the famous *Flying Dutchman*, was in these parts when a terrible storm overwhelmed him and his crew. Since there are many versions of this incident, it is difficult to have any certain opinion, but it seems that here again the Devil had a hand in this affair, ready to offer the captain his aid in exchange for the usual soul that so interests him. However, in this case God also played a role, perhaps due to the reiterated blasphemies uttered by Decken. In short, between divine wrath and ill-advised pacts, the ship ended up sinking, while its crew, by then reduced to howling shadows, were condemned to eternal, errant, and godforsaken sailing.

STARS AND FLOWERS

∾

DESPITE LYING SO NEAR TO SUCH A LARGE URBAN SPRAWL, TABLE MOUNTAIN IS STILL A HIGHLY ESTEEMED AREA OF BIO-DIVERSITY PROTECTED BY A NATIONAL PARK FOUNDED IN 1998, BOASTING ALMOST 1500 SPECIES OF PLANTS.

Fynbos is the scrub vegetation typical of this area, similar to the Mediterranean maquis but rich in endemic species. Standing out among them is protea, the plant that Linnaeus dedicated to the god Proteus, which can take on many different forms. Its flower is one of the national symbols of South Africa. Again, on the slopes of Table Mountain is the city's incredible Kirstenbosch National Botanical Garden, which is not only of unparalleled beauty but is also a precious safeguard for the study and conservation of innumerable species, some of which are endangered.

As proof of its function of acting as a link, Table Mountain is the only natural structure whose name has been given to a constellation, the Table, situated near the celestial south pole, between Hydra and Chameleon.

ARARAT

Altitude: 16,854 ft. (5137 m) a.s.l.
Prominence: 11,847 ft. (3611 m)
Topographic isolation: 235 mi. (379 km)
Coordinates: latitude 39°42'06" N; longitude 44°17'53" E
Location: the provinces of Ağrı and Iğdır

THE MOUNTAIN OF SORROW

Mount Ararat is a stratovolcano consisting of two main cones 8 miles (13 km) from each other, the Greater and Little Ararat, respectively 16,854 and 12,782 ft. (5137 and 3896 m) above sea level. In the middle fissure and on the flanks are numerous parasitic cones and cracks in the rock. The summit is covered with a cap of perennial ice that is growing smaller. There has been no documented eruptive activity recently; the larger crater is considered dormant, while the smaller one seems to be totally extinct. The slopes are rather arid and have scarce tall-stem vegetation. Lying near the borders of Turkey, Armenia, Azerbaijan, and Iran, this volcano inevitably has different names: Masis (probably in honor of King Amasya) for the Armenians, Kūh-e Nūḥ (Noah's Mountain) for the Persians, and Ağrı-Dağı (the Mountain of Sorrow) for the Turks.

The mountain is sacred for the Armenians, who consider it one of their most representative symbols, a manifestation of "wishful thinking," since it lies in current Turkish territory even though it is part and parcel of the national iconography, from literature to stamps and an unspecified number of logos and insignia. When viewing Mt. Ararat from the Armenian capital of Yerevan, one could regard it as a sort of companion that is silent and distant yet ever-present. The region around Ararat is tormented: from 1984 to 2021, except for some temporary truces, it was considered a war zone during the conflict with the Kurdish PKK separatists. All access and expeditions, even those with scientific objectives, were subject to military authorization and in any case were not safe: for example, the soldiers stationed there were allowed to shoot at persons considered illegal immigrants or even those who had wandered off the permitted routes.

BEAUTIFUL
AND IMPOSSIBLE

~

Thumbing through accounts of mountains, we almost always find more or less ancient attestation of Man's impotence when faced with such heights. This is also true of Mt. Ararat, at least according to the description made by William of Rubruck in his travel diaries dated around 1250: "Many have tried to climb it, but none has been able, and an old local explained why no one even tried: *No one must climb up to the top of Masis, because it is the mother of the world.*"

This was a question of morality and respect, more than a concrete difficulty involved in reaching the summit.

The first documented ascent took place in 1829 on the part of a strange group consisting of a German, two Russians, and three Armenians who had overestimated the height by some 328 feet (100 m) after using a mercury barometer.

VARIOUS FLOODS
AND ANOMALIES

∾

**THE BELIEF THAT HUMAN CIVILIZATION WAS STRUCK BY A TRE-
MENDOUS FLOOD AS A SORT OF BASICALLY DIVINE PUNISH-
MENT IS WIDESPREAD, FOUND IN VARIOUS WRITINGS AND
CULTURES, NOT ONLY IN THE BIBLE BUT ALSO IN BABYLONIAN
MYTHOLOGY, THE GREEK MYTH OF DEUCALION, SACRED HIN-
DU TEXTS, AND OTHERS.**

This is one of the factors that led to the opinion that a real natural catastrophe lay at the origin of these myths. And so we have the story of Noah, whose name is connected to Ararat as the possible site of the soft landing of his famous Ark. There is no certainty about this, as it seems that the remains of this floating zoo are at the very least as timid as the Loch Ness monster. Finding any order in the multiple intimations in the scriptures is no easy task, since many of them are susceptible to ambiguous interpretation, especially when it comes to finding concrete geographic evidence by reading between the lines, so to speak.

One fascinating element that participates in this debate like a sharp hatchet blow is the so-called anomaly of Mt. Ararat, a sort of unidentified object situated a mile or so from the summit at an altitude of 15,499 ft. (4724 m), which was discovered and photographed for the first time in

1949 by an American plane returning from a secret mission over the Soviet Union. This dark and elliptic shape under the frozen stratum, whose appearance is too perfect to be natural, has been identified by many as nothing more or less than a part of the Ark hull. These photographs, kept secret for decades, were followed by monitoring on the part of spy satellites—which, however, did not reveal much at all. The research expeditions attempted in the following year, which were strictly limited by the military turmoil in the zone, never succeeded in clarifying the matter, except for some sporadic and sensationalist announcement that was always controversial, such as the one of the 2010 team that claimed it had found a cavern with wooden walls dating back about 5000 years (dating certified by carbon 14) in an area that was never inhabited. This apparently remarkable discovery was immediately denied by local sources, who were sure that the wood had been placed there in plain view by a band of Kurdish jokers. Obfuscation and mysteries did not discourage the more audacious Ark searchers. On the contrary, for some of them these difficulties proved to be an even greater incentive. An example of this is the indefatigable engineer Angelo Palego, who in the 1980s devoted himself to this research and went to the mountain region no fewer than 23 times, certain he had discovered the site of the Ark. In 2021, at the age of 86, he suffered a fatal heart attack while preparing to climb the holy mountain again to establish definitive proof of his theory.

Consequently, for the moment we must admit that that old 13th-century sage was right: it is forbidden to know the truth about the mother of the world.

DAMĀVAND

Altitude: 18,405 ft. (5610 m) a.s.l.
Prominence: 15,312 ft. (4667 m)
Topographic isolation: 724 mi. (1165 km)
Coordinates: latitude 35°57'19" N; longitude 52°06'33" E
Location: Tehran, Mazandaran region

A THOUSAND RED POPPIES

We're about 43.5 miles (70 km) north of Tehran, in the middle of the Elburz range, which separates the plateau of Iran from the Caspian Sea. Mt. Damāvand dominates the surroundings, aided by its prominence, which makes it stand out even more. The snow covering the mountain shines even at night, especially in the moonlight; and at dawn its shadow captures the plateau for miles before the sun rises to liberate it. For a long time this colossal stratovolcano has been in a benevolent state of dormancy, its activity limited to having a little smoke now and again. It seems that its latest eruption dates to 7000 years ago, which is quite comforting because, judging from its size, this huge beast would be able to cause rather conspicuous damage should it decide to become active once again.

On the summit, which affords a veritable optical journey from Tehran to the southern coast of the Caspian Sea, the temperature may be below freezing even in summer, while in winter it can be as much as 70°C below zero.

The flora varies, according to the slopes and altitude, naturally, but it boasts many endemic species. Emblematic features of this vegetation are the expanses of red poppies against the form of the mountain crowned by the sky. There are also anemones and wildflowers that suddenly shoot up in spring, painting the valleys. Although the natural equilibrium of this region is threatened by sheep-farming, mining, and human settlements, it is also the home of large populations of mammals such as hedgehogs, bats, wolves, jackals, bears, foxes, deer, weasels, and lynxes, as well as marvelous raptors and various species of indigenous vipers.

SHOOTING AN ARROW

~

This commanding mountain is the ideal setting for mythological legends and stories, and naturally there is no lack of persons who identify it with one of the (many) possible landings of Noah's Ark when the Flood subsided. The symbol of solidarity and consensus, it is one of the sites that have inspired poets and authors eager to extol the pride and independence of the Persian people.

The most prominent legend regards the archer Arash, who was born in dramatic circumstances. The Persian army was defeated by the Turanian troops, and the conditions of their surrender were very severe: only the territory covered by an arrow shot would be left for the Persians. This capricious, derisive, and vaguely sadistic imposition led to the revealing of most of the archers, who knew only too well that they wouldn't be able to shoot an arrow for any considerable distance. So no one came forward, except for Arash, evidently divinely inspired. Of course, the king welcomed his courageous offer with great joy, and the archer set off for the mountains in order to find the best position to shoot from. Besides this wise stratagem, Arash performed a generous act of sacrifice, instilling his own life into the taut string of his bow. And the arrow, driven by such great energy, flew for three straight days, earning for his people a truly impressive kingdom. Naturally, since everything has its price, Arash disappeared immediately, leaving peace and prosperity in heritage to the Persians. However, it seems that his spirit continues to wander in the vicinity of Mt. Damāvand, offering comfort and aid to those who are defeated or find themselves in dire straits.

THUS SPAKE ZARATHUSTRA

∾

DAMĀVAND IS A HOLY MOUNTAIN FOR THE ZOROASTRIANS. THIS RELIGION, NAMED AFTER ITS PROPHET ZARATHUSTRA (OR ZOROASTER), IS BASED ON THE DUALISM BETWEEN THE GOOD AND EVIL THAT LIVE TOGETHER IN THE IMMORTAL SOUL OF EVERY LIVING BEING. THIS FAITH, ALTHOUGH IN DECLINE DUE TO THE MASS CONVERSION TO ISLAM—GARNISHED WITH WAVES OF PERSECUTION—WAS THE OFFICIAL RELIGION OF THE PERSIAN EMPIRE IN VARIOUS PERIODS UP TO THE 7TH CENTURY AD, AND IS STILL VERY MUCH ALIVE IN CERTAIN ZONES OF INDIA AND IRAN.

Here the Zoroastrian feast days such as the New Year, which coincides with the spring equinox and is called Nowruz, are extremely popular. The chief divinity, Ahura Mazda—creator of the sky and Earth—generated the twins Spenta Mainyu and Angra Mainyu, who represent respectively life and death, day and night, what is good and what is evil. In truth, there are different theories regarding the origin of the two rival spirits, but the point is that this inevitable struggle is reflected in the souls of individuals, who must favor Spenta with virtuous conduct. For his part, Angra Mainyu created the serpentine demon Zahāk, a three-headed dragon that unleashes storms, habitually steals livestock, and is the grim bearer of a broad gamut of misfortune. Fortunately, the warrior god Faridun, after defeating and capturing the dragon, chained it to the summit of Damāvand, where it must remain to the end of time.

NANGA PARBAT

Altitude: 26,660 ft. (8126 m) a.s.l.
Prominence: 15,118 ft. (4608 m)
Topographic isolation: 117 mi. (189 km)
Coordinates: latitude 35°14'2" N; longitude 74°35'24" E
Location: Kashmir

LIFE, DEATH, AND AMBITION

This massif rises up at the western tip of the Himalayas, where the range ends in the Indus Valley. It consists of a mass of metamorphic rock with crystalline slate and sedimentary stones, as well as material of magmatic origin. The ninth-highest peak in the world, Nanga Parbat has a very high mortality rate among those who have attempted the ascent (28%), which earned it the nickname of "killer mountain" and, in local tradition, "man-eating mountain" or "the Devil's mountain."

The first person to pay the price for his sweet obsession with this peak was Albert Frederick Mummery, born in England in 1855, a great pioneer of pure mountaineering, who used a minimum of artificial equipment. Famous for conquering Mont Blanc when only fifteen, he tended to return several times to the same mountains to open new routes and improve his knowledge of the areas. In 1895 he organized the first-ever expedition to a 26,247-foot (8000-m) summit, and did so in keeping with his philosophy, with a small group of four climbers and two porters, light gear, and the noble objective of conquering the summit of Nanga Parbat. After reaching an altitude of 20,013 ft. (6100 m), his three companions had to retreat because of altitude sickness, but Mummery refused to give in and decided to proceed together with the two Sherpas. On August 24, all traces of the three were lost, probably due to an avalanche. In the interwar period, Nanga Parbat became an objective of Nazi propaganda and was called the "German mountain of destiny." The Nazis, obsessed with the idea of planting their flag on the summit, organized various well-equipped expeditions. The 1934 ascent, led by Willy Merkl, took two mountaineers very close to the goal; but the order to wait for the rest of the team before attempting the final climb proved to be fatal. That very day, a terrific nine-day storm began, not only blocking all progress but trapping them, without food and water. In the attempt to descend, ten of the climbers died, including Merkl. In 1937, an avalanche struck the camp of a new expedition, burying 16 persons. The last attempt was made in 1939 by Aufschnaiter and Harrer, who, however, were arrested by the English at the outbreak of World War II. They succeeded in escaping from prison in India and fled to Tibet, where Harrer stayed for seven years—but this is another story, which he narrated in a famous novel. On July 3, 1953, Hermann Buhl, alone and without supplementary oxygen, reached the summit of his dreams and miraculously survived the descent after bivouacking in the open. Up to that time, 31 persons had already died during the ascent.

REINHOLD'S VERSION

~

In 1970, Reinhold Messner took part in an expedition that aimed at making the ascent via the unclimbed Rupal Face on the south end. Due to complications and differences of opinion, Reinhold chose to face the last stretch by himself, setting off before sunrise. His younger brother Günther, who had joined the team after a member withdrew, did not want to leave him alone and so followed him at a certain distance on a very steep climb and without setting up the fixed ropes for the return descent. When he reached his brother to set foot on the summit together with him, Günther was utterly exhausted and, after a makeshift bivouac, the two decided to return to the Diamir face, thus achieving the first crossing of Nanga Parbat. Günther's condition worsened with every step, but the brothers managed to overcome the worst stretch of the descent. But just when they were almost at the end, Günther, who had remained behind, was overwhelmed by an avalanche. Reinhold searched for his brother for three days but, exhausted and injured, had to give up. He was eventually saved by the local population. Severe frostbite cost him several amputations, but the greatest pain was being accused of having abandoned his brother, claims that were made by the very members of the team who had deserted the expedition. Only in 2005 was Günther's body found in a place that confirms Reinhold's account. His remains were burned, in keeping with Tibetan tradition, but Messner managed to take one of his climbing boots and some bones back home; DNA tests on the latter proved they belonged to Günther. This tragedy is the subject of the film *Nanga Parbat*.

OBSESSION

∾

AT TIMES WE FEEL THAT THE GOLDEN AGE OF MOUNTAINEERING IS SOMETHING OF THE PAST, FIRST BECAUSE EVERY CONQUEST HAS ALREADY BEEN MADE, THEN BECAUSE TECHNICAL AND TECHNOLOGICAL PROGRESS HAS MADE GIANT STEPS, BOTH IN TERMS OF GEAR, HENCE SAFETY, AND IN REGARD TO OUR KNOWLEDGE, WHICH ALLOWS FOR BETTER AND MORE STUDIED PLANNING AND GREATER PROBABILITY OF SUCCESS. ALL THIS IS TRUE, BUT THEN MAN IS, AND WILL REMAIN, TINY COMPARED TO THE POWER OF THE ELEMENTS.

That past has not really passed, and there will always be mad dreamers, gifted with courage and talent, ready to challenge the sky. Of particular topicality is the adventure of Daniele Nardi, who spoke about himself quite a lot on TV and the social media, as is normal nowadays. So we seemed to know him personally, to share a bit of his passion. Many have wondered—not always with delicacy in this jungle of computer keyboards surrounding us—how one could take such risks with a wife and a virtually newborn child at home. The answer lies suspended up there somewhere, and contains an inextricable tangle of opposing loves: the fact is, whoever feels such a strong vocation must obey the voice that is guiding him. Daniele was not a born mountaineer; on the contrary, he came from the province of Latina and discovered mountains by himself, and he loved them until he died because of them. His headstrong idea was to climb up Nanga Parbat by passing over the Mummery spur, a very risky route that many considered sheer suicide. He made several attempts, beginning in the 2012–2013 season, and something happened every time. Cold, health issues, avalanches, misunderstandings with his fellow climbers, and above all the bad weather that simply did not stop. Yes, because that route has to be taken in winter, when there is less risk of avalanches. The last attempt, which took place in 2018–2019, was no different. Daniele and Tom Ballard were there from late December to February to become acclimatized, prepare the climb, and wait for a sign of favorable weather. The delay at the base camp was long and nerve-racking; in his video, Daniele never failed to smile, but one must wonder how they passed their time there, how they managed to remain lucid and determined in those conditions. The two finally started off on February 22, successfully reaching camp 4. Then they disappeared. There followed days of anguish in which hope became increasingly feeble, until it faded away when the two bodies, wearing a red and a blue jacket, were discovered from below by means of telephoto lenses. The rescue operations were much too risky, and consequently Daniele and Tom, with the consent of their families, will remain up there forever.

LAILA PEAK

Altitude: 20,000 ft. (6096 m) a.s.l.
Prominence: 617 ft. (188 m)
Topographic isolation: not available
Coordinates: latitude 35°35'28" N; longitude 76°24'19" E
Location: Hushe Valley

A POINT IN THE SKY

We are in Karakoram, the range northwest of the Himalayas that lengthens the latter after the break of the Indus River, extending as far as Afghanistan in a sort of long natural border between China and India and Pakistani Kashmir. Excluding the North and South poles, this is the area with the highest concentration of glaciers, as well as the only region that bucks—albeit only slightly—the global trend of glacier melting and higher temperatures, an anomaly that has not yet been given a precise and convincing explanation. Laila Peak stands above the Gondogoro glacier, between Chogolisa and Masherbrum (also known respectively as Bride Peak and K1, the latter once erroneously considered the tallest mountain of Karakorum but ironically not even included among the "eight-thousanders" over 26,247 ft. [8000 m] high). Its shape is striking and captivating, a thorn piercing the sky, a nail

about to tear it in a sort of blood pact. Its crests are perfectly straight, as if someone had cut it with the skill of a master. But what makes this mountain unique is its northwest face: a spectacular ramp that descends for 4,921 ft. [1500 m] at a 45° angle, a celestial vision for those who love extreme skiing, a dream that only a very few can realize. The surrounding mountains seem to imitate its bearing, but without achieving its soaring lines, perhaps out of respect or fear. Consequently, the landscape reminds one of the exoskeleton of a prehistoric creature protected by bony plates and sharp points that will wound anything that comes too close. Curiously enough, in Pakistan there are two other mountains with the same name, one of which, in the Haramosh Valley, is almost 22,966 ft. (7000 m) high, while the other is 19,685 ft. (6000 m) in altitude and occupies the south slope of the Rupal Valley near Nanga Parbat.

UNOFFICIAL AND OFFICIAL CONQUESTS

~

In the period straddling the 1980s and 1990s, many climbs in this area were effected without the official permission of the local authorities, the lack of which made it difficult to have them recognized as bona fide ascents. The climb of Laila Peak is a case in point. In 1987, Simon Yates reached the summit together with his companions Sean Smith and Mark Miller, but could not tell anyone about this because the climb had not been authorized. Two years earlier, Yates had experienced on the Siula Grande (Peruvian Andes) the classic story one would not wish on anyone: his companion Joe Simpson had broken a leg in a fall and after Simon had helped him by slowly lowering him in stages, the two were caught in a nocturnal snowstorm. At that point, Simpson fell and remained suspended on a ledge over a crevasse, held there only by Yates's rope, which Yates had to cut to avoid being pulled down. Incredibly enough, Simpson managed to save his life and later justified Yates's terrible but necessary decision, narrating this experience in the book *Touching the Void*.

But getting back to Laila Peak, the first official ascent was made in 1997 by a group of Italians: Iacchini, Cavagnetto, Della Vedova, Ongari, and Ruggeri. On the summit, a gas cartridge bearing the names of the four Englishmen confirmed the preceding ascent of Yates, who testified to this in his autobiographical book *The Flame of Adventure*.

SKIING AND DREAMING

～

ONE CANNOT SPEAK OF LAILA PEAK WITHOUT MENTIONING SKIING. WHILE, FOR MANY, A WALL LIKE THIS COULD REPRESENT A LIVING NIGHTMARE, FOR THE FEW ADVENTURERS IT IS THE EQUIVALENT OF A DREAMLAND. ACCORDING TO THE TESTIMONY OF THOSE WHO HAVE HAD THE HONOR AND COURAGE TO MEET THE CHALLENGE, THE ATTRACTION OF AND ENTHUSIASM FOR THIS ABSOLUTELY UNIQUE ROUTE ARE IRRESISTIBLE AND CONTAGIOUS. FEAR DOES NOT EXIST, BECAUSE THIS IS THE PERFECT SLOPE. GREAT SKILL AND DETERMINATION ARE REQUIRED, BUT THIS GIVES RISE TO A SORT OF NATURAL SELECTION: IN ORDER TO REALIZE AN EXPEDITION HERE, ONE MUST FACE DIFFICULTIES THAT EXCLUDE IMPROVISERS AND TIME-WASTERS.

Unfortunately, leaving aside ability, organization, and attention to detail, luck plays a fundamental role here, and those devoted to this activity are well aware of this. In 2016, there was an expedition on the part of four young Italians: Zeno Cecon, Carlo Cosi, Enrico Mosetti, and Leonardo Comelli. Despite their ages (between 25 and 27), they were expert and well prepared: two were already alpine guides, one a ski instructor, and the last one a mountain photographer who was studying to become a guide. Their plan was ambitious but studied in great detail in order to limit the impact of misfortune and/or accidents to a minimum. The day of the ascent, after a long hike to arrive at the base camp and a pause to become acclimatized, the four arrived only 492 ft. (150 m) from the summit, but decided not to proceed because the condition of the snow seemed too risky. Despite this prudent choice, while descending, Leonardo lost control of his skis, fell for 1312 ft. (400 m) on a frozen face, and died while his friends looked on helplessly. As is always the case, there is no answer to the thousand questions that emerge after such a tragedy, except the difficult acceptance of a destiny so closely linked with passion.

In 2018, two teams managed to climb up the entire face, including the summit. In the case of the international expedition that included the mountaineer from Turin, Cala Cimenti, bad luck was the almost ludicrous fate of Julian Danzer who lost one of his skis in the precipice and had to make the downward climb with an ice-axe and crampons, missing the opportunity to make the descent he had always dreamed of. A much more tragic fate was in store for Cala, a formidable mountaineer who had climbed up Mont Blanc when he was only 12 years old and earned fame for having conquered the summit of Nanga Parbat: in 2021 an avalanche killed him at Sestriere, near his home.

K2

Altitude: 26,251 ft. (8611 m) a.s.l.
Prominence: 13,190 ft. (4020 m)
Topographic isolation: 818 mi. (1316 km)
Coordinates: latitude 35°52'57" N; longitude 76°30'48" E
Location: Pakistan and Xinjiang (China) border

A RIGHT MISTAKE

Sometimes, by chance, mistakes lead us to a broader truth; and in the case of great stories, the word "chance" becomes "destiny." The mountain known as K2 acquired this simple and modern name because at first it was considered the second-tallest peak in the Karakorum range. Later on, it was discovered that K1 was quite a bit lower, but the name K2 was kept the same, the world over. This second place does not diminish the nobility of the mountain, which is visually "more mountain" than Everest itself due to its markedly pyramidal shape and its dominating position. Of the four walls, two face the north on the Chinese side, while the others face south and belong to Pakistan. The debate over the altitude, which for some time made K2 a formidable rival of Everest, has been settled by more recent surveys; but as for the difficulty of the ascent, the roles seem to become noticeably inverted. If, as St. Thomas stated, we must see and touch in order to believe, the question is rather complicated. Yet a good compromise would be to trust those who have conquered all the eight-thousanders without oxygen, and for this we have a very reliable yardstick: Reinhold Messner is of the opinion that K2 is without a doubt the most difficult climb, taking into account the altitude, danger level, and technical difficulties. We must bear in mind that on K2, complications are to be found all along the ascent—even a short distance from the summit—while on Everest the most difficult routes are concentrated at lower altitudes. Again, there are very few places on the Savage Mountain where one can set up base camps at a high altitude. All these factors have made it the third-ranked mountain regarding the mortality rate (for every four who attempt to reach the summit, one dies), as well as the last eight-thousander to be conquered in winter—a feat achieved in 2021, more than 40 years after Everest.

THE "ITALIAN MOUNTAIN"

~

The conquest of K2 is an Italian story, followed by a train of disputes that lasted for decades and a truth impaired for years by envy, accusations, rancor, and jealousy.

The initial attempts date to the beginning of the 20th century—the 1902 ascent team included the ophthalmologist Aleister Crowley—but the most significant step was taken in 1909 by the expedition led by Luigi Amedeo di Savoia, Duke of the Abruzzi, who opened a route on the east spur of the mountain, naming it after himself. The photographer Vittorio Sella documented the feat, but the conquest of the summit still had a long way to go. In the 1930s, two attempts failed due to problems of provisioning and bad weather, and the body of the millionaire Dudley Wolfe, the first victim on this mountain, was found only in 2002. Another American expedition that took place in 1953 ended with the death of one member, Art Gilkey, who was hit by an avalanche while his companions were trying to rescue him, who was seriously ill.

But it was the following year that witnessed the controversial and heroic chapter of the conquest. The expedition was already marked by disputes before the climb even began, due to the treacherous exclusion—substantiated with false medical certificates—of such personages as Riccardo Cassin, Cesare Maestri, and Gigi Panei, great mountaineers with a character perhaps too independent for the military approach that Ardito Desio intended to give to the organization of the climb.

The large Italian team arrived in April and began a laborious period of preparation and then a long march to the Pakistani colossus. The base camp was set up above the Abruzzi Spur, at an altitude of more than 16,404 ft. (5000 m), where the 57-year-old Desio remained to coordinate the operations via radio. Setting up the camps and preparing the routes began, despite the loss of the guide from Courmayeur, Mario Puchoz, due to a pulmonary edema. With exemplary teamwork, Erich Abram, Walter Bonatti, and Ubaldo Rey managed to rig the fixed ropes on the Black Pyramid, at an altitude of about 22,966 ft. (7000 m). On July 31, Lino Lacedelli and Achille Compagnoni planted the flag on the summit for the first time, to the delight and sense of fulfillment of the Italian nation. This triumph could not tolerate negatives, so the events of the preceding night were swept under the carpet and Bonatti had to wait over 50 years before his version of the facts was verified. On July 30, while Bonatti and the local guide Amir Mahdi were engaged in taking the oxygen tanks up to camp nine as support for the final assault, Compagnoni decided to set up the camp tent higher than originally planned. When Mahdi and Bonatti arrived, they did not see anyone. By then, darkness had fallen and the wind smothered their desperate shouts, which the other two could barely hear. Lacedelli, in a tardy redefinition of the facts, postulated that Compagnoni had insisted on moving the camp because he was afraid that Bonatti would join the team during the conquest, thereby dampening the feat of the others. In any case, the result was that Mahdi and Bonatti (41 and 19 years old respectively), after having placed the oxygen tanks in plain view, were forced to dig a shelter in the snow and spend the night in the open at an altitude of 26,575 ft. (8100 m) and a temperature of 40° below zero, saving their lives only by dint of their superhuman constitution. Again, Lacedelli and Compagnoni claimed they had finished their supply of oxygen long before reaching the summit and accused Bonatti of having used some of it in order to survive without shelter, which was impossible, since the masks (fundamental to the operation of the tanks) were safely stored in their backpacks. This detail triggered heated discussions, partly because of photographs that show Compagnoni on the summit with the tank on his back and the fact that it made no sense to take empty, heavy tanks to the summit. Books have been written and documentaries made about this matter. The whole truth will probably never be known, but the in-depth research of the Italian Alpine Club's committee of specialists, undertaken in 1994 and promulgated in 2004, is very close to Bonatti's version. Now all the protagonists are resting, we hope, in peace: Amir Mahdi died in 1999, Ardito Desio at the age of 104 in 2001, Lacedelli and Compagnoni passed away in 2009, and Walter Bonatti in 2013. They all contributed to this story, to History, amidst a great deal of light and some darkness.

A CHALLENGE THAT IS STILL UNFINISHED BUSINESS

∾

TO THIS DAY, THE CLIMB UP K2 IS A VERY HIGH-LEVEL CHAL-LENGE. FROM 1954 TO 2021, ONLY 377 PERSONS REACHED THE SUMMIT, EVEN THOUGH THE INCREASE IN REQUESTS FOR AUTHORIZATION PORTENDS PROBLEMS OF CONGES-TION MUCH LIKE THOSE THAT AFFLICT MT. EVEREST. THE NU-MEROUS ACCIDENTS TESTIFY TO THE PERSISTENT EXTREME DIFFICULTY OF THE ASCENT, DESPITE TECHNICAL AND TECH-NOLOGICAL PROGRESS.

The standard pass follows the southeast ridge, above the Abruzzi Spur, and begins at an altitude of 17,700 ft. (5400 m), where a base camp can be set up at the Godwin-Austen glacier. Mountaineers must deal with the two formidable topographic features, the House Chimney and Black Pyramid, plus the steep and exposed slopes that lead to the Shoulder. The final obstacle before the summit is the Bottleneck, near the wall of seracs on the eastern part of the summit. There have been many victims of K2, no fewer than thirteen in 1986 and eleven in the space of a few hours in 2008, when more than 30 mountaineers attempted the ascent that day.

The Gilkey Memorial, a heap of stones commemorating the American mountaineer who died there in 1953, has over time become a collective mausoleum that unfortunately is continuously growing, destined to host a great number of plaques with the names of those who sacrificed their lives to this splendid and ruthless mountain.

KAILASH

Altitude: 21,778 ft. (6638 m) a.s.l.
Prominence: 4327 ft. (1319 m)
Topographic isolation: not available
Coordinates: latitude 31°04'01" N; longitude 81°18'46" E
Location: Darchen, Tibet

THE PRECIOUS JEWEL OF SNOWS

Standing out against the turquoise sky is a block of dark rock streaked with snow that becomes totally white at a higher level, a form that is only partly regular, a perfect pyramid marked by fissures that seem to be scars. In this bare and dusty stretch of Tibet, we might think we were outside the world, or even at the edge of the galaxy, but the center of the universe is right here. Mount Kailash is an unconquered summit, not because going up the slopes is prohibited by law, but out of respect for the gods. Near this mountain and the two large lakes of Manasarovar and Rakshastal are the sources of some of the longest rivers in Asia: the Sutlej, the Brahmaputra, and the Karnali (a tributary of the Ganges). This area was visited and described by the orientalist Giuseppe Tucci in 1935, when very little was known about Tibet. Here, despite the fact that going up the slopes is not allowed, there is a placid coming and going of murmuring pilgrims as well as tourists—who hopefully are respectful and driven by spiritual curiosity regarding this mountain, and who can take advantage of the help afforded by yaks to transport food, drinks, and baggage, and in some cases even ride on horses—all of whom arrive from far away by any means, even on foot if necessary. This is surprising, considering how isolated and wild this area is, with only a few austere structures and a bitterly cold and treacherous climate, not to speak of all the problems attached to high altitude. Therefore, no one comes here to challenge the mountain or conquer the summit, but rather to walk around it, paying homage to its soul and their own souls.

KORA

~

Imagine you are making your way as follows: first you kneel on the rocky terrain, then go down on all fours, and lastly lie down with your arms outstretched forward in full body prostration. Next, you get back on your feet and take a couple of steps to the point you had reached with your hands when lying down. Now you kneel again and bend until you feel the stone with your face; once again, you mark the beginning of your next step with your fingers and stand up. You repeat the process like a pendulum, gaining a bit more of the path every time. Imagine praying or singing your mantra. You are surrounded by many other persons, but this is not a race. Every so often, someone overtakes you at a leisurely pace, but this does not disturb you, nor do the pain in your joints, the fatigue, hunger, and thirst. You proceed slowly for 33.4 miles (54 km)—which will require days of effort—stopping to rest now and again at the established sites—all at an altitude of 13,123–18,372 ft. (4000–5600 m) at the Dolma Pass. This would seem to be sheer madness, yet there are so many convinced madmen that they make us begin to doubt this. This is *Kora*, the meditative experience based on a circular walk around something sacred, called *né*, while *né korwa* is the name of the pilgrim. The term used to describe this practice, circumambulation, is somewhat awkward and betrays our cultural, or at least linguistic,

limitation. Thus, the pilgrim takes a turn around Mt. Kailash, which is recommended at least once in a lifetime; while, for those who want to exaggerate, it seems that repeating this walk 108 times would guarantee the total elimination of all negative thoughts in our existence, including reincarnations. This mountain is venerated but is not climbed; merely abandoning the paths of Kora to go toward the summit is considered an extreme sacrilege, with the risk of fatal punishment, so it's better not to try. After all, it is the home of the gods, the juncture between the terrestrial and divine kingdoms, whose confines must be respected. This itinerary is followed by the faithful of the various religions that worship Kailash: Buddhists and Hindus do it clockwise, following the course of the Sun, while Jainists and the followers of Bön move in the opposite direction. Some avoid prostration but walk continuously to the end. In short, the formulas are not rigid; what counts is the purification of one's karma, which is achieved in this way. Many people also leave all their personal possessions before beginning their walks, as a sign of transformation.

BETWEEN
MYTH AND REALITY

∾

THE PILGRIMS BELONG TO FOUR RELIGIONS. HINDUS BELIEVE THAT THIS IS THE ABODE OF SHIVA, UNITED IN PERENNIAL COPULATION WITH HIS CONSORT PARVATI. BUDDHISTS CONSIDER THE MOUNTAIN THE NAVEL OF THE EARTH AND ONE OF BUDDHA'S HOMES. THE JAINISTS BELIEVE IT IS THE PLACE WHERE RISHABHA, THE FIRST OF THEIR SAINTS, ACHIEVED NIRVANA. AND FOR THE BÖN RELIGION, SIPAIMEN, THE GODDESS OF THE SKY, LIVES ON ITS SUMMIT.

Inevitably such a venerated mountain becomes a melting pot of stories, beliefs, and legends, and it enjoys the privilege of never being visited, a priceless stimulus for the imagination.

The Tibetans view it as the roof of a pagoda in the middle of a mandala representing the divine space of Demchog, where one can take the path to enlightenment and leave terrestrial passions and illusions behind. Here, on the occasion of the Saga Dawa, an important Buddhist holiday that takes place in the May–June period, a very tall flagpole with thousands of colored prayer flags is raised. The belief is that if the pole is not perfectly straight when held up, a period of misfortune will strike Tibet. Many people, including Occidentals, have tried to describe the essence of these sites, which however may be destined to remain beyond our understanding. On the other hand, we might consider it a waste of time to travel to the abode of God when we know that we won't be able to set foot there. And why should we make such a huge effort, only to discover that, when all is said and done God, is a bit everywhere, and certainly within ourselves, or that He may even be waiting for us on our sofa at home? Except that by staying at home we may not have been aware of this.

EVEREST

Altitude: 29,029 ft. (8848 m) a.s.l.
Prominence: 29,029 ft. (8848 m)
Topographic isolation: infinite
Coordinates: latitude 27°59'17" N; longitude 86°55'31" E
Location: Khumbu glacier, Nepal-China border

BECAUSE IT'S THERE

Chomolungma (Mother of the universe), *Sagaramātha* (God of the sky), or, more simply, Everest (after George Everest, a British surveyor): the highest mountain in the world, with 60 million years of history. The first (literal) victim of its fascination was George Mallory, who led many expeditions in the 1920s. His explanation of such obstinacy is famous and endearing. When asked why he insisted on climbing Everest: "Because it's there." To this day, no one knows whether he actually reached the summit. What is certain is that his body lay 820 feet (250 m) from the summit from his death in June 1924 to 1999, when it was finally found. Although the most accredited hypothesis is that he died before completing the ascent, the fact that the photograph of his wife he had taken with him was missing leaves room for the romantic theory that he

had left it on the peak, as he had intended. Be that as it may, Mt. Everest was officially conquered in 1953 by Edmund Hillary (later Sir) and Tenzing Norgay, who decided not to reveal which one had first set foot on the summit. Tenzing, who at first seemed to be rather nondescript, turned out to be an extremely fascinating person. Of more than humble origins, during his childhood he moved from Tibet to Nepal, became a porter, and then, thanks to his skills, was an active member of many expeditions, enjoying fame and influence after the Everest exploit. Curiously enough, his birthday coincides with the date of the celebrated climb, and not by chance: he himself chose it, since he didn't know when he had been born, which seems to be 1914, the Tibetan Year of the Rabbit. Hillary and Tenzing searched in vain for some sign of the passage of Mallory and his companion, Irvine. For his part, Tenzing left the flags of the UN, Great Britain, India, and Nepal on the summit, as well as biscuits and chocolate for the gods, a package of candy, a doll in the shape of a cat, and two of his daughter's pencils. Since then, this mountain has witnessed records of all kinds, becoming the aspiration of many—even too many—expeditions. Jon Krakauer's book *Into Thin Air* narrates the 1996 tragedy that cost the lives of eight climbers, victims of exposure after a huge storm that caught three parties by surprise at the same time, which highlights risks due to inefficient organization and a superficial approach, problems that have only worsened.

THIN AIR FOR SURE

~

Nowadays, everything is more accessible, even Everest. We have lost track of that healthy fear that at times saves our lives—and fingers and toes. Given the relative proportions, here again we have the now-classic and widespread example of people roving about in many Western mountain areas wearing thongs. Accessibility in itself is not a drawback, but here it has a many-sided boomerang effect. Sudden changes in the weather are never gentle, nor can they be foretold; and the cold and—above all—the altitude are challenging, even for the strongest constitutions.

This is partly a subjective matter, since every body reacts in its own way; but there is a limit, a warning whistle, known as the death zone, beyond which the human organism cannot become acclimatized and can only survive for a certain length of time while the cells begin to die. Furthermore, altitude hypoxia conditions our cognitive faculties, influencing our capacity to make the right decisions. Although the altitude may cause serious problems even at much lower levels, it is a fact that no organism can exist at an altitude of over 26,247 feet (8000 m) for long—in some cases, days, but at times a few hours too many can be fatal.

A record of those who died on Everest is longer than a pre-pandemic shopping list. Some deaths are marked by a touch of heroism, while others seem so tragically stupid and banal as to make one wonder whether all this is worthwhile. A case in point is the number of deaths caused by climbers having to wait for hours to make the ascent. In May 2019, there was a maximum of 200 arrivals in one day, with people remaining immobile for more than two hours—a situation caused by disorganization and by the money-making business of issuing permits, considering the fact that the time available to make a climb is rather short.

On the other hand, the story of Francys Distefano and Sergei Arsentiev, which took place in May 1998, has the flavor of a Shakespearean tragedy. This Russian and his American wife were very much in love and, above all, united by their profound love of mountaineering. She wanted to become the first American woman to reach the summit without supplemental oxygen, and he wanted to help her realize this dream, no matter what. Two problems forced them to postpone the summit attempt, and at that stage it would have been wiser to call it quits; but so many hours spent at that high altitude had befogged their brains. Betrayed partly also by their exceptional energy, the couple managed to reach the summit on the third day, by then battered by the altitude. During their return, made at night, they became separated unwittingly and Sergei realized this only once he reached their tent. Francys had collapsed on her side at an altitude of 28,215 feet (8600 m), still alive but delirious and unable to move. Another expedition passing by the next morning tried to help her, but she was convulsing. In the meantime, her husband went back up to look for her. This may seem banal, but for someone who has been at an altitude of more than 26,247 feet (8000 m) for days, this requires a super-human effort. Yet what the body cannot achieve, love can: Sergei managed to reach her, aware that this was the end for both of them. Another night passed, wrapped in mystery, but most probably the couple spent it next to each other. The following morning, the mountaineer Ian Woodall and his wife Cathy stopped to help Francys, who was already in her death throes. Of Sergei there remained only his ice axe, a bit of rope, and his tracks toward the abyss. They could do nothing for her and, weighing the value of life, were forced to leave her and return safely to the camp, their souls wounded by what they had seen. Nine years later, Ian took part in a very special expedition whose objective was not to conquer the world's highest summit, but rather to retrieve Francys's body, which had remained frozen in the same place, exposed to the gaze of anyone passing by. This was no mean feat, for most of the corpses of those who succumb to the rigors of the altitude—not to speak of the victims of falls or avalanches—remain there, and retrieving them is too risky. Many people have died while attempting to do so, in a macabre vicious circle.

RICHES AND RAGS

∾

RIGHT HERE, ON THE TALLEST PEAK IN THE WORLD, A PLACE WE WISH COULD BE CONSIDERED SACRED EVEN FOR NON-BELIEVERS—A SORT OF SANCTUARY OF NATURE AND RE-SPECT—THERE IS TANGIBLE PROOF OF HOW HATEFUL HUMANS CAN BE, PARASITES ABLE TO TRANSFORM ANYTHING THEY TOUCH INTO A CESSPOOL, LIKE A KING MIDAS OF DUNG.

It has been estimated that about 600 persons per year reach the summit, which on average requires spending a couple of months at the three acclimatization camps. Each of these persons, without counting all the related commercial spin-off, produces an amount of refuse we can only imagine, plus all the excrement left in the snow. Our consciousness has grown, projects such as the one aimed at transforming garbage into art works will help, but this is certainly not enough to curb the phenomenon, which is now one of the many ecological emergencies for which only we are to blame. Then there is global warming, which with a certain sense of humor gradually revives all the lovely memories we thought we had left in the snow for good—which is no laughing matter.

AMA DABLAM

Altitude: 22,349 ft. (6812 m) a.s.l.
Prominence: 3369 ft. (1027 m)
Topographic isolation: not available
Coordinates: latitude 27°51'39" N; longitude 86°51'39" E
Location: Khumbu Himal Valley,
Sagarmatha National Park

THE MOTHER'S NECKLACE

We live in difficult times. We must constantly show how excited we are on social media, while at the same time experiencing a sense of anesthesia, a routine of being on the go that grinds our emotions and leaves them insipid. We see almost everything via a screen, and that "everything" is already déjà vu and banal. But it really needn't be so: little is required to rediscover enchantment and marvel, which is like an uppercut that nullifies all faculty of expression. Hopefully, that is what will happen when you see the eyes of a person that make your heart beat faster, the iris with those tiny nuances that vary constantly while remaining the same; it will happen with your favorite poem or song that you hear by chance on the radio. And the same is true of a mountain. You will find yourself thinking that this is the most beautiful mountain in the world, that there is nothing more—yes, the word "beautiful" is almost unoriginal, but after

having considered all the other possible words in the dictionary you will choose it, the simplest one. You will be amazed at how this sense of the marvelous can repeat itself, how a phrase like "the most beautiful mountain," which by definition is false and impossible, is at the same time true. You will use parabolic comparisons, just as poets once called upon their muses for help: for example, when face to face with Ama Dablam, you cannot help thinking of Mont Blanc. Indeed, this mountain is known as the Mont Blanc of Himalaya due to its similar shape, but perhaps its real name is more appropriate. Mother's Necklace refers to the long ridges on either side that look like arms, giving the impression that the central part is a woman's neck and that the mountain, despite its austere appearance, represents an embrace and protection. An illustrious neighbor is Mt. Everest, which enjoys a special visual contact with Ama Dablam.

A CLANDESTINE CONQUEST

~

The story of the first ascent of this mountain has its special features, but in order to avoid misunderstandings it must be pointed out that the first two attempts, made in 1958 and 1959, failed tragically. While in the first case the rope team gave in to bad weather and the difficulties of the southwest face at 19,685 feet (6000 m), in the second things went even worse because the British mountaineers Michael Harris and George Fraser disappeared just before reaching the summit. The 1961 ascent had other objectives, the main one being to study the reaction of the human organism to high altitude. The leader of this team was a certain Edmund Hillary. In fact, the first person to conquer Mt. Everest was the head of this expedition but was at that moment in the United States giving a series of lectures, after which he intended to join his companions in Nepal. However, despite the fascinating observation of a local pilgrim who always slept outdoors at 15° below zero without gloves or a sleeping bag or even winter clothing, the group soon abandoned their study, bewitched by the fascination of Ama Dablam. Nothing could deter them, not winter, much less the fact that they lacked the permission to make the ascent. On March 13, the New Zealanders Mike Gill and Wally Romanes, the American Barry Bishop, and the Englishman Mike Ward planted their ice axes on the top of the splendid woman. However, their impeccable mountaineering feat had serious consequences: the Nepalese government vehemently threatened to sue and punish them for their disrespectful childish prank. Only the arduous mediation of Sir Hillary, who at first risked being expelled before even getting off the airplane, managed to save the day after many humble apologies and paying a fine of sixty dollars.

ONE PLACE, TWO WORLDS

❧

A FASCINATING VIEWPOINT OF THIS MOUNTAIN, ITS HISTO-
RY, AND THE DIFFERENT PERCEPTION BETWEEN THE LOCAL
POPULATIONS AND THOSE WHO ARRIVE FROM ABROAD, IS
PRESENTED IN THE FILM *HOLY MOUNTAIN,* DIRECTED BY REIN-
HOLD MESSNER. BASING THE FILM ON A TRUE STORY, THE
GREAT MOUNTAINEER FROM BRESSANONE USES IT TO PAINT
THE OVERALL PICTURE OF A THRILLING AND TRAGIC EVENT
THAT OCCURRED IN 1979. REINHOLD WAS IN THE BASE CAMP,
TOGETHER WITH PHYSICIAN OSWALD ÖLZ, WHEN A GROUP
OF FOUR MOUNTAINEERS ON A FACE WAS STRUCK BY A HUGE
BLOCK OF ICE THAT HAD FALLEN OFF A SERAC.

Three of the climbers survived but were injured and in a desperate situation on a spur of rock. Due to a strange quirk of destiny, one of them is Peter Hillary, the son of the world famous Sir Edmund. The documentary describes a daring and exciting rescue operation, together with a representation of the history of the mountain. The Sherpa population departed from the eastern section of Tibet together with 20,000 yak and succeeded in arriving at Khumbu Valley; consequently they consider this mountain holy, and their interpretation and judgment of the behavior and activity of Westerners is based in this light. The disappearance of the first explorers who attempted the ascent was a clear sign from the mountain, which did not tolerate being violated. Another episode was considered a curse: this time Peter Hillary was paying for the offenses of his father, who was responsible for the expedition that had climbed up Ama Dablam without authorization, triggering exemplary punishment. The reconstruction of the rescue, with Simon Messner playing the role of his father (even wearing the very same clothing his father had worn then), shows both sides of the story without being judgmental, thus adhering to the principle that a fine and powerful story always contains something edifying and does not need explicit didacticism or a moral.

FUJI

Altitude: 12,388 ft. (3776 m) a.s.l.
Prominence: 12,388 ft. (3776 m)
Topographic isolation: 1291 mi. (2077 km)
Coordinates: latitude 35°21'48" N; longitude 138°43'34" E
Location: Honshu Island, border of the Shizuoka
and Yamanashi prefectures

INFINITE VIEWS OF THE INCOMPARABLE

One has the sensation that it is the background of every image of Japan, with the same silent, discreet presence of an authoritative father who remains at a certain distance but is and will always be there, whatever should happen.

This is the holy mountain of Japan, and the tallest one, visible even from the skies of Tokyo, which is about 62 miles (100 km) away, and is imprinted on one's mind, partly thanks to the 36 views created by Hokusai. Fuji is a stratovolcano surrounded by five lakes that, despite the popular tradition depicting it as having come into being suddenly because of an earthquake in 286 BC, was formed gradually by the lava that flowed in four very intense phases of eruptive activity. Its present appearance should be dated to 10,000 years ago. It lies right at the spot where the Philippine Plate is descending beneath the Eurasian plate, tectonic movement that creates a large magma reservoir in depth, where molten rock lies before eruption. The latest eruption, known as Hōei, dates to 1707 and lasted more than two weeks, covering even present-day Tokyo in a thick layer of ashes. Despite its tapered and regular shape, so proverbial in iconography, Fuji boasts a wealth of crests, crevices, and caves created by the lava flow and the following action of wind, snow, and water erosion. The pure and abundant water here is a great resource for the area, useful for the inhabitants and local industries, as well as the animals and plants. The Shiraito Falls, 66 ft. (20 m) high and 219 yards (200 m) wide, emerge from a long cleft between two layers of lava and feed the Shiba River. The climate on the summit is bitterly cold, and snow usually covers the peak for ten months every year and sometimes falls in July and August as well.

PILGRIMS

~

There are a great many holy mountains in Japan, but Mt. Fuji is certainly the most important one. In an ancient Japanese proverb, which has several versions, the number of ascents is clearly stated: "There are two kinds of madmen: those who do not climb up Mt. Fuji at least once, and those who try to do so a second time." The first person to make this pilgrimage was the Buddhist monk En No Gyōja in 663. For a very long time, women were prohibited from making the ascent, although it seems that some did so anyway by wearing men's clothing. And it was precisely this kind of transgression on the part of Fanny Parkes, the wife of a British diplomat who went to the summit of Fuji in 1867, which sparked the process of change. The gods don't bother about such occurrences as eruptions, earthquakes, or various types of disparity, nor did humans find the matter so improper, so that in the space of five years the prohibition was abolished, along with a series of reforms that led Japan to modernize itself and emerge from feudalism during the Meiji period, the so-called enlightened reign. Nowadays the mountain can be visited by pilgrims in the months of July and August.

THE MOUNTAIN
AND THE MOON

∾

MOUNT FUJI HAS INSPIRED MANY STORIES, EACH OF WHICH IN TURN HAS MANY VERSIONS, CREATING A CERTAIN AMOUNT OF LEEWAY OF INTERPRETATION. THE STORY OF KAGUYA-HIME (*THE TALE OF THE BAMBOO CUTTER*) IS A GREAT FAVORITE AMONG THE JAPANESE, WHO HAVE AN INTIMATE AND MYSTICAL CONCEPTION OF BEAUTY AND ARE USED TO CONTEMPLATING THE MOON OR CHERRY-TREE BLOSSOMS THAT MANIFEST ABOVE ALL THE EPHEMERAL NATURE OF THIS EXPLOSION OF COLOR.

The bamboo cutter and his wife had been married for some time and had no children despite their continuous prayers. One day, the cutter came upon a large bamboo stalk, where he discovered a tiny and delicate creature, a baby girl only a few inches long but extremely beautiful and radiant. The cou-ple, by now elderly, could not believe this good fortune and immediately adopted the child with no questions asked. What's more, during the following days the bamboo cutter found a gold nugget in every plant he cut, so that the family became rich in no time. Worried that all this was too good to be true, the couple enjoyed their new fate with discretion and protected their daughter—who in the meantime had grown up quickly and was now a beautiful woman, obviously different from any other creature—from the pitfalls of the rest of the world. However, they could not stop rumors and gossip from spreading, and soon suitors began to arrive from all over Japan to ask for her hand, but she immediately turned them down. Then five princes arrived one day to woo her, and Kaguya-hime promised she would marry the one who would bring her one of five objects, objects so rare that they had to give up trying and even die while trying. The emperor himself fell in love with her, but she gently refused. Only at that point did Kaguya-hime reveal to her parents that she came from the Moon and could not marry a human being. She was a true blessing for her parents; but after their death, which was imminent, she had to return to her moon. After hearing this sad prophecy, the emperor tried to stop her with the aid of his army, but all she did was to give him a mirror that he could use to see her every so often. The emperor, mad with sorrow, followed her as far as possible, to the top of Mt. Fuji, until he dropped the mirror, which began to burn, which is the reason why the mountain continues to spew its smoke toward the Moon, where Kaguya-hime lives, at an unreachable distance. In other versions, Kaguya-hime offered the emperor the elixir of life, but the ending is similar: the emperor rejected a life, even eternal life, without his love, and so he tossed the precious elixir into the volcano, and only a plaintive wisp of smoke rose up toward our silver satellite.

ULURU
(or AYERS ROCK)

Altitude: 2831 ft. (863 m) a.s.l.
Prominence: 1142 ft. (348 m)
Topographic isolation: not available
Coordinates: latitude 25°20'42" S; longitude 131°02'10" E
Location: Uluru-Kata Tjuta National Park

THE TIP OF THE ICEBERG

In this trip around the world, we have seen this many a time: there's no one way to be a mountain, every mountain is such in its own way. The common denominator is the energy they succeed in emanating in their total silence, the contemplative and spiritual respect they impart in those who observe them. On the whole, the mountain seems to know something about that sensation of seeing something but intuiting much more, that famous "essential invisible to the eyes" the old Saint Exupéry spoke of, and it whispers this to you in a language you manage to grasp without understanding the details.

So here we are: Uluru is yet another mountain without a pointed peak or a high altitude, yet it is capable of being so striking and extraordinary, as if it were the navel of the world. It is not only the infinite bush country surrounding it that bows down before this mountain up to the last horizon, thus underscoring its dominion, yet it is clear that there is much more to it. In fact, the monolith we see is a small part of an immense block of sandstone that lies below in the earth for a depth of 4.3 miles (7 km), a block that also includes other ranges as far away as 15 miles (25 km). Uluru, named Ayers Rock by the colonists, has a circumference of 5.6 miles (9 km) and is surrounded by precipitous faces about 1148 feet (350 m) high. Thanks to the high percentage of iron in its minerals, Mount Uluru offers marvelous plays of light and, especially at dawn and sunset, acquires hues that vary from ochre to bronze by way of violet, bright red, and rust.

ANCESTRAL MYTHS

~

Scattered here and there on the rocks of Uluru are rupestral paintings that the Yankunytjatjara and Pitjantjatjara aboriginals consider holy. They are redone periodically, but some date back thousands of years. They are scenes of ancient myths depicting the stories of Dreamtime, connected to the origin of the world. The Dreamtime is a sort of Big Bang in which the ancestral gods acquire the form of living animal and vegetal beings and then go on to create the Earth, with its seas, lakes, rivers, and mountains. The last to be created is Man, who is entrusted with the task of looking after the works of the gods. Although many of these legends are kept secret and are not revealed to the *piranypa* (non-Aboriginals), some are known. For example, the serpent, after crossing an arid desert, decided to plant a gigantic seed in order to originate life. The intention was to grow a large tree in whose shade both plants and animals would flourish. In order to do this, the serpent invoked heavy rainfall, but the seed remained sterile, as it was too large to germinate and with time became hard red rock—Mount Uluru.

Here, more or less every mark, every spot or crack, has an explanation: be it the blood of the serpent Liru, guilty of having stolen the eggs of the pythoness Kuniya, or the holes in the rock that a huge red lizard made in its efforts to find the boomerang it had thrown against the mountain and lost.

A BITTER TRUTH

∽

ON AUGUST 17, 1980, THERE OCCURRED A SCANDAL, A REAL-LY NASTY BUSINESS, THAT AROUSED THE MORBID CURIOSI-TY OF THE PUBLIC FOR QUITE SOME TIME: TWO-MONTH-OLD AZARIA CHAMBERLAIN DISAPPEARED INTO OBLIVION WHILE ON A CAMPING TRIP WITH HER FATHER AND MOTHER UNDER MT. ULURU. THE MOTHER WAS ACCUSED OF INFANTICIDE AND TRIED, BUT FOR THE MEDIA SHE WAS ALREADY GUILTY AND WAS LITERALLY CRUCIFIED.

This incident cost the mother three years in prison and many more years to fight for her reputation even after finally being absolved: according to a court of appeals, a dingo had taken and killed the child. And according to a Dreamtime legend, it was a dingo that had exterminated the entire population of this area to punish it for having participated in a feast with an enemy tribe.

In truth, the Aboriginals had tried for years and years to have climbing on the sacred mountain prohibited; but since this would have had a negative impact on the tourism industry, the natives were forced to witness the daily profanation of their holy site on the part of hundreds of noisy visitors who went up and down the rock like so many ants sporting outlandish clothing, with the aid of a handhold that was added to facilitate the climb, a feat that is certainly not impossible but not without its risks, given the steep gradient and above all the high temperature and ruthless sun. In fact, many foreigners have died of heart attacks in this region. Since 2019, climbing on Uluru has been prohibited, in a tardy process of redemption on the part of the "white" population that to a certain degree has restored dignity and freedom of choice to the local populations.

PHOTO CREDITS

page 9 Eugene Ga/Shutterstock

pages 10-11 Sakarin Sawasdinaka/Shutterstock

page 12 Jnjphotos/Shutterstock

page 15 Enn Li Photography/Moment/Getty Images

page 17 Steve Allen/Shutterstock

page 20 Jason Chu/500px/Getty Images

page 23 Bruce Heinemann/Stockbyte/Getty Images

page 24 Matt Kazmierski/Moment/Getty Images

page 27 C. Fredrickson Photography/Moment/Getty
Images

pages 28-29 Phitha Tanpairoj/Shutterstock

page 31 Dancestrokes/Shutterstock

page 32 Alexandree/Shutterstock

pages 34-35 Jonathan Murrish/EyeEm/Getty Images

page 36 davidluna/RooM/Getty Images

page 39 Martin Harvey/The Image Bank/Getty
Images

page 40 Galyna Andrushko/Shutterstock

page 43 Mono Andes/Moment Open/Getty Images

pages 44-45 Giulio Ercolani/Alamy Stock Photo

page 47 Galyna Andrushko/Shutterstock

page 48 SL-Photography/Shutterstock

page 51 Markus Daniel/Moment Open/Getty Images

page 53 Adwo/Shutterstock

pages 54-55 Markus Daniel/Moment/Getty Images

page 56 AIDE PAULMICHL/500px/Getty Images

page 59 Nataliya Hora/Shutterstock

pages 60-61 Olga Gavrilova/Shutterstock

page 63 Marisa Estivill/Shutterstock

page 64 Ana Luisa Correa/500px/Getty Images

pages 66-67 Gambarini Gianandrea/Shutterstock

page 68 Curioso.Photography/Shutterstock

page 71 A.Pushkin/Shutterstock

pages 72-73 Javier Ghersi/Moment/Getty Images

page 75 Milosz Maslanka/Shutterstock

page 76 SinghaphanAllB/Moment/Getty Images

page 78 borchee/E+/Getty Images

page 81 Laurie Noble/Stone/Getty Images

pages 82-83 Ratnakorn Piyasirisorost/Moment/Getty
Images

page 84 Patrick Möhl, Switzerland/Moment/Getty
Images

page 87 imageBROKER/Alamy Stock Photo

page 89 Dmytro Tymchenko/Shutterstock

page 90 Michal Ludwiczak/Shutterstock

page 91 Graphene/Shutterstock

pages 92-93 O.C Ritz/Shutterstock

page 94 Prisma by Dukas/Universal Images Group/
Getty Images

page 97 Nedjat Nuhi/Shutterstock

pages 98-99 Francesco Costa

page 101 Francesco Costa

pages 102-103 georgeclerk/E+/Getty Images

page 104 Bkrzyzanek/Shutterstock

page 107 Roberto Moiola/Sysaworld/Moment/Getty
Images

page 108 Oleg Senkov/500px/Getty Images

pages 110-111 travelwild/Shutterstock

page 113 AlbertoSimonetti/E+/Getty Images

page 114 Lubo Ivanko/Shutterstock

page 117 Chris Whiteman/Alamy Stock Photo

pages 118-119 WLDavies/E+/Getty Images

page 121 Martin Harvey/The Image Bank/Getty
Images

page 122 Kanuman/Shutterstock

page 125 Shawn Levin/Shutterstock

pages 126-127 Martin Harvey/DigitalVision/Getty
Images

page 129 Peter Unger/Stone/Getty Images

page 130 Whatafoto/Shutterstock

page 133 Naeblys/Shutterstock

pages 134-135 James Strachan/Photodisc/Getty Images

page 137 Kamil Can YILMAZ/Shutterstock

page 138 Photo by Zahra Mandana Fard, baraneh.com/Moment/Getty Images

page 141 Deev Lab/EyeEm/Getty Images

pages 142-143 Yasaman Jalali/EyeEm/Getty Images

page 145 Abbas Yousefshahi/Shutterstock

page 146 Pakawat Thongcharoen/Shutterstock

page 149 Francesco Costa

page 150 Patrick Poendl/Shutterstock

page 153 Feng Wei Photography/Moment Open/Getty Images

pages 154-155 Galen Rowell/Corbis Documentary/Getty Images

page 156 Pornchai_Ar/Shutterstock

page 158 Punnawit Suwattananun/Shutterstock

pages 160-161 Thrithot/Shutterstock

page 163 Punnawit Suwuttananun/Moment/Getty Images

page 164 Pornchai_Ar/Shutterstock

page 166 Nadeem Khawar/Moment Open/Getty Images

page 169 Hussain Warraich/Shutterstock

pages 170-171 Kitti Boonnitrod/Moment/Getty Images

page 173 Patrick Poendl/Shutterstock

page 174 msiudmak/Shutterstock

page 177 luyao/Shutterstock

page 178 Mikhail Vinnikov/500px/Getty Images

page 181 ShuHo/Shutterstock

pages 182-183 Storm Is Me/Shutterstock

page 184 JohanSjolander/E+/Getty Images

pages 186-187 Francis Cassidy/Alamy Stock Photo

page 188 John Harper/Stone/Getty Images

page 191 Kitti Boonnitrod/Moment/Getty Images

page 193 Didier Marti/Moment/Getty Images

page 194 hadynyah/E+/Getty Images

page 196 Ryan C Slimak/Shutterstock

pages 198-199 Sergej Onyshko/Shutterstock

page 201 Daniel Prudek/Shutterstock

pages 202-203 Olga Gavrilova/Shutterstock

page 204 Grant Faint/The Image Bank/Getty Images

page 206 DoctorEgg/Moment/Getty Images

pages 208-209 yongyuan/E+/Getty Images

page 211 patthamapong/Shutterstock

pages 212-213 Dmitry Morgan/Shutterstock

page 214 structuresxx/Shutterstock

page 217 Ted Mead/The Image Bank Unreleased/Getty Images

pages 218-219 bmphotographer/Shutterstock

page 221 Travelscape Images/Alamy Stock Photo

Cover: Viaframe/Stone/Getty Images

NICOLA BALOSSI RESTELLI

~

Nicola Balossi Restelli is an author born in Milan, where he lives with his wife and children. An aficionado of mountains, folklore, and sports, he has contributed articles to online magazines and blogs. He also works for various publishers, some of which have published his stories and essays.